Informing the legislative debate since 1914

Small Business Size Standards: A Historical Analysis of Contemporary Issues

Robert Jay Dilger
Senior Specialist in American National Government

January 3, 2014

Congressional Research Service

7-5700

www.crs.gov

R40860

CRS REPORT
Prepared for Members and
Committees of Congress

Summary

Small business size standards are of congressional interest because the standards determine eligibility for receiving Small Business Administration (SBA) assistance as well as federal contracting and tax preferences. Although there is bipartisan agreement that the nation's small businesses play an important role in the American economy, there are differences of opinion concerning how to define them. The Small Business Act of 1953 (P.L. 83-163, as amended) authorized the SBA to establish size standards for determining eligibility for federal small business assistance. The SBA currently uses two types of size standards to determine SBA program eligibility: industry-specific size standards and alternative size standards based on the applicant's maximum tangible net worth and average net income after federal taxes.

The SBA's industry-specific size standards determine program eligibility for firms in 1,047 industrial classifications in 18 sub-industry activities described in the North American Industry Classification System (NAICS). The size standards are based on one of the following four measures: number of employees, average annual receipts in the previous three years, average asset size as reported in the firm's four quarterly financial statements for the preceding year, or a combination of number of employees and barrel per day refining capacity. Overall, the SBA currently classifies about 97% of all employer firms as small. These firms represent about 30% of industry receipts.

The SBA has always based its size standards on economic analysis of each industry's overall competitiveness and the competitiveness of firms within each industry. However, in the absence of precise statutory guidance and consensus on how to define small, the SBA's size standards have often been challenged, typically by industry representatives seeking to increase the number of firms eligible for assistance and by Members concerned that the size standards may not adequately target assistance to firms that they consider to be truly small.

During the 111th Congress, P.L. 111-240, the Small Business Jobs Act of 2010, authorized the SBA to establish an alternative size standard using maximum tangible net worth and average net income after federal taxes for both the 7(a) and 504/CDC loan guaranty programs. It also established, until the SBA acted, an interim alternative size standard for the 7(a) and 504/CDC programs of not more than $15 million in tangible net worth and not more than $5 million in average net income after federal taxes (excluding any carry-over losses) for the two full fiscal years before the date of the application. It also required the SBA to conduct a detailed review of not less than one-third of the SBA's industry size standards every 18 months.

This report provides a historical examination of the SBA's size standards, and assesses competing views concerning how to define a small business. It also discusses H.R. 585, the Small Business Size Standard Flexibility Act of 2011, which would have authorized the SBA's Office of Chief Counsel for Advocacy to approve or disapprove a size standard proposed by a federal agency if it deviates from the SBA's size standards. The SBA's Administrator currently has that authority. It also discusses P.L. 112-239, the National Defense Authorization Act for Fiscal Year 2013, which requires the SBA to make available a justification when establishing or approving a size standard that the size standard is appropriate for each individual industry classification. It addresses the SBA's recent practice of combining size standards within industrial groups as a means to reduce the complexity of its size standards and to provide greater consistency for industrial classifications that have similar economic characteristics.

Contents

What Is a Small Business?... 1
How Big Is Small?... 3
Who Makes the Call?... 4
Early Definitions of Small Business Vary in Approach and Criteria... 5
The Small Business Act of 1953's Definition of Small Provides Room for Interpretation 7
Industry Challenges the SBA's Initial Size Standards, Claiming They Are Too Restrictive 8
GAO and Several Members of Congress Challenge the SBA's Size Standards, Claiming
    They Are Too Broad 10
SBA Proposes More Restrictive Size Standards Based on Industry Competitiveness 12
SBA Proposes to Streamline its Size Standards... 16
SBA Adopts a More Incremental, Targeted Approach... 18
Congress Requires Periodic Size Standard Reviews 22
SBA's Definitions for Small Business 27
    Alternative Size Standards.. 28
    Industry Size Standards 29
    Other Federal Agency Size Standards 33
Congressional Policy Options.. 35

Tables

Table 1. Number of Employer Firms, Employer Firm Employment, and Employer Firm
    Annual Payroll, by Employer Firm Employment Size, 2011 3
Table 2. Industry-Based Size Standard Levels Currently Being Applied During the SBA's
    On-going Review of its Size Standards 20
Table 3. Status of SBA Size Standard Reviews, 2010-2013 24

Contacts

Author Contact Information... 37

What Is a Small Business?

There is bipartisan agreement that small businesses play an important role in the American economy.[1] However, there are differences of opinion concerning how to define them. This issue is of congressional interest because the definition used determines business eligibility for Small Business Administration (SBA) assistance as well as federal contracting and tax preferences.

The Small Business Act of 1953 (P.L. 83-163, as amended) authorized the SBA and justified the agency's existence on the grounds that small businesses are essential to the maintenance of the free enterprise system.[2] In economic terms, the congressional intent was to use the SBA to deter the formation of monopolies and the market failures monopolies cause by eliminating competition in the marketplace.

The Small Business Act of 1953 provides the SBA authority to establish size standards for determining eligibility for federal small business assistance. The SBA currently uses two types of size standards to determine SBA program eligibility: industry-specific size standards and alternative size standards based the applicant's maximum tangible net worth and average net income after federal taxes. The SBA's industry-specific size standards are also used to determine eligibility for federal small business contracting purposes.

The SBA's industry-specific size standards determine program eligibility for firms in 1,047 industrial classifications (hereinafter industries) in 18 sub-industry activities described in the North American Industry Classification System (NAICS). Given its mandate to promote competition in the marketplace, the SBA has based its size standards on an economic analysis of each industry's overall competitiveness and the competitiveness of firms within the industry.[3] The size standards are based on the following four measures: number of employees, average annual receipts in the previous three years, average asset size as reported in the firm's four quarterly financial statements for the preceding year, or a combination of number of employees and barrel per day refining capacity. Overall, the SBA currently classifies about 97% of all employer firms as small.[4] These firms represent about 30% of industry receipts.

As will be discussed, the SBA began a comprehensive size standards review in 2008. At that time, the SBA used 41 different size standards: number of employees (7 size standards), average annual

---

[1] Senate Democratic Policy Committee, "Senate Democrats Are Committed to America's Small Businesses," Washington, DC: Senate Democratic Policy Committee, May 18, 2009, at http://sbc.senate.gov/DPC_small_biz_doc.pdf; Senate Republican Policy Committee, "Taxing Success: President Obama's Tax Increases on Small Businesses are Bad for Job Creation," Washington, DC: Senate Republican Policy Committee, March 17, 2009, at http://rpc.senate.gov/public/_files/031709TaxingSuccess.pdf; and President Barack Obama, "Remarks by the President to Small Business Owners, Community Lenders and Members of Congress," press release, Office of the Press Secretary, March 16, 2009, at http://www.whitehouse.gov/the_press_office/Remarks-by-the-President-to-small-business-owners/. For further analysis of the role of small businesses in job creation, see CRS Report R41392, *Small Business and the Expiration of the 2001 Tax Rate Reductions: Economic Issues*, by Jane G. Gravelle and Sean Lowry.

[2] P.L. 83-163, the Small Business Act of 1953, §202.

[3] U.S. Small Business Administration, Office of Government Contracting and Business Development, "SBA Size Standards Methodology," April 2009, p. 1, at http://www.sba.gov/sites/default/files/size_standards_methodology.pdf.

[4] U.S. Small Business Administration, "SBA's Size Standards Analysis: An Overview on Methodology and Comprehensive Size Standards Review," power point presentation, Khem R. Sharma, SBA Office of Size Standards, July 13, 2011, p. 4, at http://www.actgov.org/sigcom/SIGs/SIGs/SBSIG/Documents/2011%20-%20Documents%20and%20Presentations/Size%20Stds%20Presentation_SIG%20Meeting.pdf.

receipts in the previous three years (31 size standards), average assets (1 size standard), annual megawatt hours of electric output in the preceding fiscal year (1 size standard), and a combination of number of employees and barrel per day refining capacity (1 size standard). It also had 11 other size standards for its financial and other programs.

Since 2008, the SBA has used eight receipt-based size standards and eight employee-based size standards when establishing new, or reviewing existing, size standards. The SBA has argued that reducing the number of receipt-based size standards, from 31 to 8, will simplify the management and use of size standards and provide "greater consistency in size standards among industries that are similar in their economic characteristics."[5]

In the absence of precise statutory guidance and consensus on how to define small, the SBA's size standards have often been challenged, typically by industry representatives seeking to increase the number of firms eligible for assistance. The size standards have also been challenged by Members of Congress concerned that the size standards may not adequately target federal assistance to firms that they consider to be truly small.

During the 111th Congress, P.L. 111-240, the Small Business Jobs Act of 2010, authorized the SBA to establish an alternative size standard using maximum tangible net worth and average net income after federal taxes for both the 7(a) and 504/CDC loan guaranty programs. It also established, until the SBA acted, an interim alternative size standard for the 7(a) and 504/CDC programs of not more than $15 million in tangible net worth and not more than $5 million in average net income after federal taxes (excluding any carry-over losses) for the two full fiscal years before the date of the application.[6] It also required the SBA to conduct a detailed review of not less than one-third of the SBA's industry size standards every 18 months beginning on the date of enactment of the new law (September 27, 2010).

This report provides a historical examination of the SBA's size standards and assesses competing views concerning how to define a small business. It also discusses H.R. 585, the Small Business Size Standard Flexibility Act of 2011, which would have authorized the SBA's Office of Chief Counsel for Advocacy to approve or disapprove a size standard proposed by a federal agency if it deviates from the SBA's size standards. The SBA's Administrator currently has that authority. Under current practice, the SBA's Administrator, through the SBA's Office of Size Standards, consults with the SBA's Office of Advocacy prior to making a final decision on such requests.

This report also discusses P.L. 112-239, the National Defense Authorization Act for Fiscal Year 2013, which became law on January 2, 2013. It requires the SBA when establishing or approving a size standard to make available a justification that the size standard is appropriate for each individual industry classification within a grouping of four-digit NAICS codes. It addresses the

---

[5] U.S. Small Business Administration, Office of Government Contracting and Business Development, "SBA Size Standards Methodology," April 2009, p. 22, at http://www.sba.gov/sites/default/files/size_standards_methodology.pdf.

[6] On December 20, 2010, the SBA announced that it planned to issue a notice of proposed rulemaking concerning the new alternative size standard in February 2011. It did not do so. On January 8, 2013, the SBA announced that it would issue an interim final rule, to be effective when published, establishing an alternative size standard for the 7(a) and 504/CDC programs by October 2013. See U.S. Small Business Administration, "Small Business Jobs Act: Small Business Size Standards; Alternative Size Standard for 7(a) and 504 Business Loan Programs," 75 *Federal Register* 79868, December 20, 2010 and U.S. Small Business Administration, "Small Business Jobs Act: Small Business Size Standards; Alternative Size Standard for 7(a) and 504 Business Loan Programs," 78 *Federal Register* 1638, January 8, 2013. The SBA also indicated in its notice of proposed rulemaking on January 8, 2013, that "the amendments will increase the current alternative standard for applicants for 504 loans."

SBA's recent practice of combining size standards within industrial groups to provide greater consistency for industries that have similar economic characteristics.[7]

How Big Is Small?

There were an estimated 28.2 million businesses in the United States in 2011, including about 5.7 million employer firms and 22.5 million nonemployer firms.[8] Nonemployer firms have no paid employees, annual business receipts of $1,000 or more ($1 or more in the construction industries), and are subject to federal income tax.[9] Most nonemployers are self-employed individuals operating very small unincorporated businesses, which may or may not be the owner's principal source of income. These firms are excluded from most business statistics.[10]

As **Table 1** indicates, in 2011 (the latest available data) there were 5,684,424 employer firms in the United States employing 113,425,965 people and providing total payroll of $5.16 trillion.

Table 1. Number of Employer Firms, Employer Firm Employment, and Employer Firm Annual Payroll, by Employer Firm Employment Size, 2011

Number of Employees	Number of Employer Firms	Cumulative Percentage of Total Number of Employer Firms	Employment	Cumulative Percentage of Employer Firm Total Employment	Employer Firm Annual Payroll ($1,000)	Cumulative Percentage of Employer Firm Total Annual Payroll
0-4a	3,532,058	62.1%	5,857,662	5.2%	$230,422,086	4.5%
5-9	978,993	79.3%	6,431,931	10.8%	$218,085,669	8.7%
10-19	592,963	89.8%	7,961,281	17.9%	$284,251,614	14.2%
20-99	481,496	98.3%	18,880,001	34.5%	$746,085,051	28.6%
100-499	81,243	99.8%	15,867,437	48.5%	$690,509,553	42.0%
500-999	8,761	99.9%	6,060,684	53.8%	$280,489,990	47.4%
1,000-1,999	4,368	99.9%	6,086,182	59.2%	$301,705,244	53.3%
2,000-4,999	2.703	99.9%	8,365,242	66.6%	$443,817,772	61.9%
5,000+	1,839	100.0%	37,915,545	100.0%	$1,969,530,926	100.0%
Total	5,684,424		113,425,965		$5,164,897,905	

---

[7] U.S. Small Business Administration, "Small Business Size Standards: Professional, Scientific and Technical Services," 76 *Federal Register* 14327, March 16, 2011.

[8] U.S. Census Bureau, "Statistics of U.S. Businesses: U.S. & States, totals," at http://www.census.gov/econ/susb/index.html; and U.S. Census Bureau, "Nonemployer Statistics," at http://censtats.census.gov/cgi-bin/nonemployer/nonsect.pl.

[9] U.S. Census Bureau, "Nonemployer Statistics: Definitions," at http://www.census.gov/econ/nonemployer/definitions.htm.

[10] U.S. Census Bureau, "Nonemployer Statistics," at http://www.census.gov/econ/nonemployer/index.html. Nonemployer firms account for less than 4% of business annual sales or receipts.

Source: U.S. Census Bureau, "U.S. Census Bureau, "Statistics of U.S. Businesses: U.S. & States, totals," at http://www.census.gov/econ/susb/index.html; and "U.S. Census Bureau, "Statistics of U.S. Businesses: U.S., NAICS sectors, large employment sizes" at http://www.census.gov/econ/susb/index.html.

a. Employment is measured in March, thus some employer firms (start-ups after March, closures before March, and seasonal firms) will have zero employment and some annual payroll.

Most employer firms (62.1%) had 4 or fewer employees, 89.8% had fewer than 20 employees, 98.3% had fewer than 100 employees, and 99.8% had fewer than 500 employees in 2011. The table also provides data concerning three possible economic factors that might be used to define a small business: an employer firm's number of employees as a share (cumulative percentage) of the total number of employer firms, as a share of employer firm total employment, and as a share of employer firm total annual payroll.

As will be discussed, the SBA has traditionally applied economic factors to specific industries, not to cumulative statistics for all employer firms, to determine which firms are small businesses. Nonetheless, the data in **Table 1** illustrate how the selection of economic factors used to define small business affects the definition's outcome. For example, for illustrative purposes only, if the mid-point (50%) for these three economic factors was used to define what is a small business, three different employee firm sizes would be used to designate firms as small:

- Businesses would be required to have less than 5 employees to be defined as small if the definition for small used the mid-point (50%) share of the total number of employer firms (employer firms with four or fewer employees accounted for 62.1% of the total number of employer firms in 2011).

- Businesses would be required to have less than 1,000 employees to be defined as small if the definition for small used the mid-point (50%) share of employer firm total employment (employer firms with less than 1,000 employees accounted for 53.8% of employer firm total employment in 2011).

- Businesses would be required to have less than 2,000 employees to be defined as small if the definition for small used the mid-point (50%) share of employer firm total annual payroll (employer firms with less than 2,000 employees accounted for 53.3% of employer firm total annual payroll in 2011).

Other economic factors that might be used to define a small business include the value of the employer firm's assets or its market share, expressed as a firm's sales revenue from that market divided by the total sales revenue available in that market or as a firm's unit sales volume in that market divided by the total volume of units sold in that market.

Who Makes the Call?

The Small Business Act of 1953 (P.L. 83-163, as amended) authorized the SBA to establish size standards for determining eligibility for small business assistance. More than 55 years have passed since the SBA established its initial small business size standards on January 1, 1957.[11] Yet, decisions made then concerning the rationale and criteria used to define small businesses established precedents that continue to shape current policy. Moreover, as mentioned previously,

---

[11] U.S. Small Business Administration, "Part 103 - Small Business Size Standards," 21 *Federal Register* 9709-9714, December 7, 1956.

since its beginnings the SBA has based its size standards on economic analysis of each industry's overall competitiveness and the competitiveness of firms within each industry. However, in the absence of precise statutory guidance and consensus on how to define small, the SBA's size standards have often been challenged, typically by industry representatives seeking to increase the number of firms eligible for assistance and by Members of Congress concerned that the size standards do not adequately target the SBA's assistance to firms that they consider to be truly small.

Over the years, the SBA typically reviewed its size standards piecemeal, reviewing specific industries when the SBA determined that an industry's market conditions had changed or the SBA was asked to undertake a review by an industry claiming that its market conditions had changed. On five occasions, in 1980, 1982, 1992, 2004, and 2008, the SBA proposed a comprehensive revision of its size standards. The SBA did not fully implement any of these proposals, but the arguments presented, both for and against the proposals, provide a context for understanding the SBA's current size standards, and the rationale and criteria that have been presented to retain and replace them. In addition, as mentioned previously, P.L. 111-240, the Small Business Act of 2010, requires the SBA to conduct a detailed review of not less than one-third of the SBA's industry size standards during the 18-month period beginning on the date of enactment (September 27, 2010) and during every 18-month period thereafter.[12]

Early Definitions of Small Business Vary in Approach and Criteria

There is no uniform or accepted definition for a small business. Instead, several criteria are used to determine eligibility for small business spending and tax programs.[13] This was also the case when Congress considered establishing the SBA during the early 1950s. For example, in 1952, the House Select Committee on Small Business reviewed federal statutes, executive branch directives, and the academic literature to serve as a guide for determining how to define small businesses.

The Select Committee began its review by asserting that the need to define the concept of small business was based on a general consensus that assisting small business was necessary to enhance economic competition, combat monopoly formation, inhibit the concentration of economic power, and maintain "the integrity of independent enterprise."[14] It noted that the definition of small businesses in federal statutes reflected this consensus by taking into consideration the firm's size relative to other firms in its field and "matters of independence and nondominance."[15] For example, the War Mobilization and Reconversion Act of 1944 defined a small business as either

---

[12] P.L. 111-240, the Small Business Act of 2010, §1344. Updated Size Standards.

[13] According to one source, the Internal Revenue Code contains at least 24 different definitions of a small business. See Douglas K. Barney, Chris Bjornson, and Steve Wells, "Just How Small Is Your Business?," *The National Public Accountant*, August 2003, pp. 4-6, at http://findarticles.com/p/articles/mi_m4325/is_2003_August/ai_n25073718/, cited in CRS Report RL32254, *Small Business Tax Benefits: Current Law and Main Arguments For and Against Them*, by Gary Guenther.

[14] U.S. Congress, House Select Committee on Small Business, *Review of Small Business: 82nd Congress*, final report pursuant to H.Res. 33, A Resolution Creating a Select Committee to Conduct a Study and Investigation of the Problems of Small Business, 82nd Cong., 2nd sess., December 31, 1952 (Washington: GPO, 1952), pp. 5, 13, 14, 78, and 136.

[15] Ibid., p. 3.

"employing 250 wage earners or less" or having "sales volumes, quantities of materials consumed, capital investments, or any other criteria which are reasonably attributable to small plants rather than medium- or large-sized plants."[16] The Selective Service Act of 1948 classified a business as small for military procurement purposes if "(1) its position in the trade or industry of which it is a part is not dominant, (2) the number of its employees does not exceed 500, and (3) it is independently owned and operated."[17]

The Select Committee also found that, for data-gathering purposes, the executive branch defined small businesses in relative, as opposed to absolute, terms within specific industries. For example, the Bureau of Labor Statistics "defined small business in terms of an average for each industry based on the volume of employment or sales. All firms which fall below this average are deemed to be small."[18] The U.S. Census Bureau also used different criteria for different industries. For example, manufacturing firms were classified as small if they had fewer than 100 employees, wholesalers were considered small if they had annual sales below $200,000, and retailers were considered small if they had annual sales below $50,000. According the Census Bureau, in 1952, small businesses accounted for "roughly 92 percent of all business establishments, 45 percent of all employees, and 34 percent of all dollar value of all sales."[19]

The Select Committee also noted that in 1951, the National Production Authority's Office of Small Business proposed defining all manufacturing firms with less than 50 employees as small and any with more than 2,500 employees as large. Manufacturers employing between these numbers of employees would be considered large or small depending on the general structure of the industry to which they belonged. The larger the percentage of total output produced by large firms, the larger the number of employees a firm could have to be considered small. Using this definition, most manufacturing firms with less than 50 employees would be classified as small, but others, such as an aircraft manufacturer, could have as many as 2,500 employees and still be considered small.[20]

For procurement purposes, the Select Committee found that executive branch agencies defined small businesses in absolute, as opposed to relative, terms, using 500 employees as the dividing line between large and small firms. Federal agencies defended the so-called 500 employee rule on the grounds that it "had the advantage of easy administration" across federal agencies.[21]

In reviewing the academic literature, the Select Committee reported that Abraham Kaplan's *Small Business: Its Place and Problems* defined small businesses as those with no more than $1 million in annual sales, $100,000 in total assets, and no more than 250 employees. Applying this

---

[16] Ibid., p. 2.

[17] Ibid; and U.S. Congress, Conference Committee, *Selective Service Act of 1948*, conference report no. 2438, 80th Cong., 2nd sess., June 19, 1948 (Washington: GPO, 1948), p. 24.

[18] U.S. Congress, House Select Committee on Small Business, *Review of Small Business: 82nd Congress*, final report pursuant to H.Res. 33, A Resolution Creating a Select Committee to Conduct a Study and Investigation of the Problems of Small Business, 82nd Cong., 2nd sess., December 31, 1952 (Washington: GPO, 1952), p. 3.

[19] Ibid.

[20] Ibid., p. 4.

[21] U.S. Congress, House Select Committee on Small Business, Subcommittee No. 2, *Definition of "Small Business" Within Meaning of the Small Business Act of 1953, as Amended*, hearing on H.Res. 114, 84th Cong., 2nd sess., July 5, 1956 (Washington: GPO, 1956), p. 19.

definition would have classified about 95% of all business concerns as small, and would have accounted for about half of all nonagricultural employees.[22]

Based on its review of federal statutes, executive branch directives, and the academic literature, the Select Committee decided that it would not attempt "to formulate a rigid definition of small business" because "the concept of small business must remain flexible and adaptable to the peculiar needs of each instance in which a definition may be required."[23] However, it concluded that the definition of *small* should be a relative one, as opposed to an absolute one, that took into consideration variations among economic sectors:

> This committee is also convinced that whatever limits may be established to the category of small business, they must vary from industry to industry according to the general industrial pattern of each. Public policy may demand similar treatment for a firm of 2,500 employees in one industry as it does for a firm of 50 employees in another industry. Each may be faced with the same basic problems of economic survival.[24]

The Small Business Act of 1953's Definition of Small Provides Room for Interpretation

Reflecting the view that formulating a rigid definition of small business was impractical, the Small Business Act of 1953 provided leeway in defining small businesses. It defined a small firm as "one that is independently owned and operated and which is not dominant in its field of operation."[25] The SBA was authorized to establish and subsequently alter size standards for determining eligibility for federal programs to assist small business, some of which are administered by the SBA.[26] The act specifies that the size standards "may utilize number of employees, dollar volume of business, net worth, net income, a combination thereof, or other appropriate factors."[27] It also notes that the concept of small is to be defined in a relative sense, varying from industry to industry to the extent necessary to reflect "differing characteristics" among industries.[28]

---

[22] U.S. Congress, House Select Committee on Small Business, *Review of Small Business: 82nd Congress*, final report pursuant to H. Res. 33, A Resolution Creating a Select Committee to Conduct a Study and Investigation of the Problems of Small Business, 82nd Cong., 2nd sess., December 31, 1952 (Washington: GPO, 1952), p. 4. See Abraham David Hannath Kaplan, *Small Business: Its Place and Problems* (NY: McGraw-Hill Book Co., 1948), pp. 21, 22.

[23] U.S. Congress, House Select Committee on Small Business, *Review of Small Business: 82nd Congress*, final report pursuant to H.Res. 33, A Resolution Creating a Select Committee to Conduct a Study and Investigation of the Problems of Small Business, 82nd Cong., 2nd sess., December 31, 1952 (Washington: GPO, 1952), p. 4.

[24] Ibid., p. 5.

[25] 15 U.S.C. §632(a)(1).

[26] Initially, the SBA size standards applied only to its own programs. Other federal agencies used the SBA size standards for procurement purposes on a voluntary basis. The Regulatory Flexibility Act of 1980 directed federal agencies to use SBA size standards or establish their own definitions after conferring directly with the SBA's Bureau (now Office) for Advocacy. U.S. Congress, Senate Committee on Small Business, *Small Business Administration's Size Standards*, hearing, 97th Cong., 1st sess., May 5, 1981 (Washington: GPO, 1981), p. 18. Also, see 5 U.S.C. §601(3).

[27] 15 U.S.C. §632(a)(2).

[28] 15 U.S.C. §632(a)(3).

The House Committee on Banking and Currency's report accompanying H.R. 5141, the Small Business Act of 1953, issued on May 28, 1953, provided the committee's rationale for not providing a detailed definition of small:

> It would be impractical to include in the act a detailed definition of small business because of the variation between business groups. It is for this reason that the act authorizes the Administration to determine within any industry the concerns which are to be designated small-business concerns for the purposes of the act.[29]

The report did not provide specific guidance concerning what the committee might consider to be small, but it did indicate that data on industry employment, as of March 31, 1948, "reveals that on the basis of employment, small business truly is small in size. Of the approximately 4 million business concerns, 87.4% had under 8 employees and 95.2% of the total number of concerns, employed less than 20 people."[30]

Industry Challenges the SBA's Initial Size Standards, Claiming They Are Too Restrictive

Initially, the SBA created two sets of size standards, one for federal procurement preference and set-aside programs and another for the SBA's loan and management training services. At the request of federal agencies, the SBA adopted the then-prevailing small business size standard used by federal agencies for procurement, which was 500 or fewer employees. The SBA retained the right to make exceptions to the 500 or fewer employee procurement size standard if the SBA determined that a firm having more than 500 employees was not dominant in its industry.

For the SBA's loan and management training services, the SBA's staff reviewed economic data provided by the Census Bureau to arrive at what Wendell Barnes, SBA's administrator, described at a congressional hearing in 1956 as "a fairly accurate conclusion as to what comprises small business in each industry."[31] Jules Abels, SBA's economic advisor to the administrator, explained at that congressional hearing how the SBA's staff determined what constituted a small business:

> There are various techniques for the demarcation lines, but in a study of almost any industry, you will find a large cluster of small concerns around a certain figure.... On the other hand, above a certain dividing line you will find relatively few and as you map out a picture of an industry it appears that a dividing line at a certain point is fair.[32]

On January 5, 1956, the SBA published a notice of proposed rulemaking in the *Federal Register* announcing its first proposed small business size standards.[33] During the public comment period, representatives of several industries argued that the proposed standards were too restrictive and

---

[29] U.S. Congress, House Committee on Banking and Currency, *Small Business Act of 1953*, report to accompany H.R. 5141, 83rd Cong., 1st sess., May 28, 1953, H.Rept. 83-494 (Washington: GPO, 1953), p. 3.

[30] Ibid., p. 4.

[31] U.S. Congress, House Select Committee on Small Business, Subcommittee No. 2, *Definition of "Small Business" Within Meaning of the Small Business Act of 1953, as Amended*, hearing on H. Res. 114, 84th Cong., 2nd sess., July 5, 1956 (Washington: GPO, 1956), p. 24.

[32] Ibid., p. 39.

[33] U.S. Small Business Administration, "Small Business Size Standards," 21 *Federal Register* 79-80, January 5, 1956.

excluded too many firms. In response, Mr. Abels testified that the SBA decided to adjust its figures to make them "a little bit more liberal because there was some feeling on the part of certain industries that they were too tight and that they excluded too many firms."[34] The SBA published its final rule concerning its small business size standards on December 7, 1956, and they became effective on January 1, 1957.[35]

The SBA decided to use number of employees as the sole criterion for determining if manufacturing firms were small and annual sales or annual receipts as the sole criterion for all other industries. Mr. Abels explained at the congressional hearing the SBA's rationale for using number of employees for classifying manufacturing firms as small and annual sales or annual receipts for all other firms:

> in the absence of automation which would give one firm in an industry a great advantage over another, roughly speaking if the firms were mechanized to the same extent, a firm with 400 employees would have an output which would be twice as large as the output of a firm with 200 employees.... However when you depart from the manufacturing field and go into, say, a distributive field or trade, it then becomes necessary to discard the number of employees, because it is a matter of judicial notice, that one man for example in the distributive trades can sell as much as 100 men can sell. One small construction firm possibly can do a lot more business than one with a lot more employees. A service trade again has its volume geared to something other than the number of employees. So I think that one can say with reasonable certainty that it is only within the manufacturing field that the employee standard is the uniform yardstick, but that other than manufacturing the dollar volume is the appropriate yardstick.[36]

The SBA's initial size standards defined most manufacturing firms employing 250 or fewer employees as small. In addition, the SBA considered manufacturing firms in some industries (e.g., metalworking and small arms) as small if they employed 500 or fewer employees, and in some others (e.g., sugar refining and tractors) as small if they employed 1,000 or fewer employees. To be considered small, wholesalers were required to have annual sales volume of $5 million or less; construction firms had to have average annual receipts of $5 million or less over the preceding three years; trucking and warehousing firms had to have annual receipts of $2 million or less; taxicab companies and most firms in the service trades had to have annual receipts of $1 million or less; and most retail firms had to have annual sales of $1 million or less.[37]

Mr. Abels testified that the SBA experienced "continual" protests of its size standards by firms denied financial or support assistance because they were not considered small. He also testified that in each case, the SBA denied the protest and determined, in his words, that the standard was "valid and accurate."[38]

---

[34] U.S. Congress, House Select Committee on Small Business, Subcommittee No. 2, *Definition of "Small Business" Within Meaning of the Small Business Act of 1953, as Amended*, hearing on H. Res. 114, 84th Cong., 2nd sess., July 5, 1956 (Washington: GPO, 1956), p. 40.

[35] U.S. Small Business Administration, "Part 103 - Small Business Size Standards," 21 *Federal Register* 9709-9714, December 7, 1956.

[36] Ibid., p. 41.

[37] Ibid., p. 3. In the retail sector, department and variety stores, grocery stores with fresh meats, and new and used automobile stores were considered small if they had annual sales volume of $2 million or less. In the service trades sector, hotels and power industry firms were considered small if they had annual receipts of $2 million or less.

[38] Ibid., p. 40.

The SBA also experienced some opposition to its decision to adopt the then-prevailing 500 or fewer employee size standard for all industries for federal procurement preference and set-aside programs. For example, Irvin Maness, subcommittee counsel for the Select Committee on Small Business Subcommittee No. 2, argued during a congressional oversight hearing in 1956 that the SBA's use of the so-called rule of 500 employees as the size standard for procurement violated congressional intent, which he argued was to have a definition for small business that varied "on an industry-to-industry basis."[39] Several Members also objected to the possibility that some firms could be considered small for procurement purposes, but not for the SBA's loan and management training services.

GAO and Several Members of Congress Challenge the SBA's Size Standards, Claiming They Are Too Broad

In 1977, the U.S. General Accounting Office (GAO, now the U.S. Government Accountability Office) was asked by the Select Committee on Small Business to review the SBA's size standards. At that time, most of the SBA's size standards remained at their original 1957 levels, other than a one-time upward adjustment for inflation in 1975 for industries using annual sales and receipts to restore eligibility to firms that may have lost small-business status due solely to the effect of inflation.[40]

GAO's report, issued in 1978, noted that the SBA's regulations indicated that the SBA used the following factors in formulating its size standards:

- because the purpose of SBA assistance is to preserve free competitive enterprise by strengthening the competitive position of small business concerns, the size standards should be limited to the segment of each industry that is struggling to become or remain competitive;

- because smaller concerns often are forced to compete with middle-sized as compared with very large concerns, the standard for each industry should be established as low as reasonably possible; and

- small businesses should not rely on continuing assistance but should plan for the day when they will be able to compete without assistance.[41]

---

[39] Ibid., pp. 33, 43.

[40] U.S. Congress, House Committee on Small Business, Subcommittee on General Oversight and Minority Enterprise, *Size Standards for Small Business*, hearing, 96th Cong., 1st sess., July 10, 1979 (Washington: GPO, 1979), p. 3. GAO reported that adjustments to the size standards had been made to "only 81 of the 534 industries covered by the special standards" from January 1, 1968 through April 25, 1978. The upward inflation adjustments for industries using annual sales or receipts ranged from 10.3% to 92.9% depending on the date when the standards were adopted. See U.S. Small Business Administration, "Small Business Size Standards," 40 *Federal Register* 24210-24215, June 5, 1975, and U.S. Small Business Administration, "Small Business Size Standards Regulation," 40 *Federal Register* 32824-32826, August 5, 1975.

[41] U.S. General Accounting Office, *What Is A Small Business? The Small Business Administration Needs To Reexamine Its Answer*, CED-78-149, August 9, 1978, pp. 1, 2, at http://www.gao.gov/assets/130/123644.pdf.

After conducting its analysis, GAO found that the SBA's size standards "are often high and often are not justified by economic rationale."[42] Specifically, GAO reported that

> many size standards may not direct assistance to the target group described in SBA regulations as businesses "struggling to become or remain competitive" because the loan and procurement size standards for most industries were established 15 or more years ago and have not been periodically reviewed; SBA records do not indicate how most standards were developed; and the standards often define as small a very high percentage of the firms in the industries to which they apply.[43]

GAO recommended that the SBA reexamine its size standards "by collecting data on the size of bidders on set-aside and unrestricted contracts, determining the size of businesses which need set-aside protection because they cannot otherwise obtain Federal contracts" and then consider reducing its size standards or "establishing a two-tiered system for set-aside contracts, under which certain procurements would be available for bidding only to the smaller firms and others would be opened for bidding to all businesses considered small under present standards."[44]

Citing the GAO report, several Members objected to the SBA's size standards at a House Committee on Small Business oversight hearing conducted on July 10, 1979. Representative John J. LaFalce, chair of the House Committee on Small Business Subcommittee on General Oversight and Minority Enterprise, stated that "what we have faced from 1953 to the present is virtually nothing other than acquiescence to the demands of the special interest groups. That is how the size standards have been set."[45] Representative Tim Lee Carter, the subcommittee's ranking minority Member, stated that "it seems to me that we may be fast growing into just a regular bank forum not just to small business but to all business."[46] At that time, approximately 99% of all firms with employees were classified by the SBA as a small business.[47]

Roger Rosenberger, SBA's associate administrator for policy, planning and budgeting, testified at the hearing that the SBA would undertake a comprehensive economic analysis of industry data to determine if its size standards should be changed. However, he also defended the validity of the SBA's size standards, arguing that the task of setting size standards was a complicated and difficult one because of "how market structure and size distribution of firms vary from industry to industry."[48] He testified that some industries are dominated by a few large firms, some are comprised almost entirely of small businesses, and others "can be referred to as a mixed industry."[49] He argued that each market structure presents unique challenges for defining small businesses within that industry group. For example, he argued that it was debatable whether the

---

[42] Ibid., p. 3.

[43] Ibid.

[44] Ibid., p. 20.

[45] U.S. Congress, House Committee on Small Business, Subcommittee on General Oversight and Minority Enterprise, *Size Standards for Small Business*, hearing, 96th Cong., 1st sess., July 10, 1979 (Washington: GPO, 1979), p. 9.

[46] Ibid., p. 6.

[47] U.S. Congress, Senate Committee on Small Business, *Small Business Administration's Size Standards*, hearing, 97th Cong., 1st sess., May 5, 1981 (Washington: GPO, 1981), p. 14.

[48] U.S. Congress, House Committee on Small Business, Subcommittee on General Oversight and Minority Enterprise, *Size Standards for Small Business*, hearing, 96th Cong., 1st sess., July 10, 1979 (Washington: GPO, 1979), p. 17.

[49] Ibid.

SBA should provide any assistance to any of the businesses within industries where "smaller firms are flourishing."[50] He added that

> We have no problem identifying either the very small firms or the large firms, in any given industry. Our problem is with that gray area–the so-called mid-sized firm. Should the mid-sized firm be included or excluded based on the competitive aspects of the market? Should we assist competition in an industry by aiding the mid-sized firms, since they probably represent the only major competitive force vis-a-vis the dominant companies given that these firms may also compete with the very small firms?[51]

SBA Proposes More Restrictive Size Standards Based on Industry Competitiveness

On March 10, 1980, the SBA issued a notice of proposed rulemaking for "a substantial revision of its size standards."[52] In an effort to "simplify SBA programs for the small business community, reduce administrative complexity, and increase the effectiveness of SBA programs by improved targeting of its resources," the SBA proposed to replace its two sets of size standards, one for procurement preference and set-aside programs and another for its loan and consultative support services, with a single set of size standards for both purposes.[53]

The SBA also proposed to use a single factor, the firm's number of employees, for definitional purposes for nearly all industries instead of using the firm's number of employees for some industries, the firm's assets for others, and the firm's annual gross receipts for still others. The SBA argued that

> when size standards are denominated in dollars, i.e., annual revenues, its ability to help the small business sector is undermined by inflation. Using employment, as opposed to dollar sales, will provide greater stability for SBA and its clients; will remove inter-industry distortions generated by differential inflation rates; and reduce the need for SBA to make frequent revisions in the size standards merely to reflect price increases.[54]

In setting its proposed new size standards for each industry (ranging from 15 or fewer employees to 2,500 or fewer employees), the SBA first placed each industry into one of three groups: concentrated, competitive, or mixed. Concentrated industries are "characterized by a highly unequal distribution of sales among the firms in the industry, e.g., the four largest firms accounting for more than half the industry's sales."[55] Competitive industries "display a more equal distribution of sales, and the average firm is relatively small when measured by annual sales or number of employees."[56] In competitive industries, the four largest firms typically account for less than 20% of industry sales. Mixed industries do not "meet the criteria of competitive or

---

[50] Ibid., p. 28.

[51] Ibid.

[52] U.S. Congress, House Committee on Small Business, *Small Business Size Standards*, hearing, 96th Cong., 2nd sess., March 13, 1980 (Washington: GPO, 1980), p. III.

[53] Ibid., p. 49.

[54] Ibid., p. 50.

[55] Ibid., p. 48.

[56] Ibid.

concentrated industries."[57] In mixed industries, the four largest firms typically account for 20% to 50% of industry sales.[58]

The SBA determined that there were 160 concentrated industries, 317 competitive industries, and 249 mixed industries.[59] The SBA argued that establishing a size standard for the 160 concentrated industries was a "straight-forward task—simply identify and exclude those few firms which account for a disproportionately large share of the industry's sales."[60] For competitive industries, the SBA argued that the size standard should be set "relatively low, so as to support entry and moderate growth."[61] The SBA argued that mixed industries require "relatively high size standards ... to reinforce competition and offset the pressures to increase the degree of concentration in these industries."[62]

The proposed new SBA size standards would have had the net effect of reducing the number of firms classified as small by about 225,000.[63] In percentage terms, the number of firms classified as small would have been reduced from about 99% of all employer firms to 96%.[64]

Over 86% of the more than 1,500 public comments received by the SBA concerning its proposed new size standards criticized the proposal. Most of the criticism was from firms that would no longer be considered small under the new size standards.[65] In addition, several federal agencies indicated that the proposed size standards in the services and construction industries were set too low, reducing the number of small firms eligible to compete for procurement contracts below levels they deemed necessary to ensure adequate competition to prevent agency costs from rising. They also argued that the proposed size standards would reduce the number of firms eligible to compete for procurement contracts that are "sufficiently large to perform the majority of [procurement] set-aside programs."[66] For example, the Department of Defense argued that "the small business firms must have the infrastructure both capitalwise and employeewise to compete in this particular area. They cannot be 'Mom and Pop Shops' which some of the proposed size standards [would require]."[67] It also argued that in the services area "the receipt of the very first contract would automatically make many small business firms large business. We think that is wrong."[68]

On October 21, 1980, Congress provided additional time to consider the consequences of the proposed changes to the size standards by adopting the Small Business Export Expansion Act of

---

[57] Ibid.

[58] U.S. Congress, Senate Committee on Small Business, *Small Business Administration's Size Standards*, hearing, 97th Cong., 1st sess., May 5, 1981 (Washington: GPO, 1981), p. 19.

[59] U.S. Congress, House Committee on Small Business, *Small Business Size Standards*, hearing, 96th Cong., 2nd sess., March 13, 1980 (Washington: GPO, 1980), p. 48.

[60] Ibid., p. 49.

[61] Ibid.

[62] Ibid.

[63] U.S. Congress, Senate Committee on Small Business, *Small Business Administration's Size Standards*, hearing, 97th Cong., 1st sess., May 5, 1981 (Washington: GPO, 1981), p. 11.

[64] Ibid., p. 25.

[65] Ibid., pp. 4, 10, 16.

[66] Ibid., pp. 21, 43.

[67] Ibid., p. 43.

[68] Ibid., p. 44.

1980 (P.L. 96-481). It prohibited "the SBA from promulgating any final rule or regulation relating to small business size standards until March 31, 1981."[69] In the meantime, the Reagan Administration entered office, and, as is customary when there is a change in Administration, replaced the SBA's senior leadership.

The SBA's new administrator, Michael Cardenas, praised the previous (Carter) Administration's efforts to (1) apply a comprehensive rationale (based on industry competitiveness), as opposed to a piecemeal approach, for determining the SBA size standards; (2) adopt a single size standard as a means to prevent the possibility of firms qualifying for procurement preferences, but not for the SBA's loan and consultative support services; and (3) increase the reliance on the firm's number of employees, as opposed to its annual sales and receipts, for most industries as a means to avoid having to update the size standards to reflect inflation.[70] However, he was sympathetic to the concerns of federal agencies that the proposed size standards in the services and construction industries were set too low to meet those agencies' procurement needs. As a result, he indicated that the SBA would modify its size standards proposal by increasing the proposed size standards for 51 industries, mostly in the services and construction industries. He also indicated that the proposed size standards in 157 manufacturing industries would be lowered (typically from 2,500 or fewer employees to 500 or fewer employees) to prevent one or more of the largest producers in those industries from being classified as small. He also increased the SBA's proposed lowest size standard from 15 or fewer employees to 25 or fewer employees. This change would have affected 93 service and trade industries. He testified on May 5, 1981, before the Senate Committee on Small Business, that these changes

> have the net effect of restoring approximately 60,000 firms to eligibility out of a total of 225,000 firms (including farms) that had been removed from eligibility in the advance notice. Since the SBA estimates that there are at present a total of 7.3 million firms in the United States (based on Bureau of the Census data), the proposed changes actually impact on only a small proportion of firms in the economy.[71]

The SBA did not formally issue a notice of proposed rulemaking concerning its new size standards proposal. Instead, for more than a year, it met with various trade organizations and federal agency procurement officials to discuss the proposal. As these consultations took place, the SBA experienced turnover in its senior leadership.

The SBA, headed by the new appointee, James C. Sanders, issued a notice of proposed rulemaking concerning its size standards on May 3, 1982. Mr. Sanders testified before the House Committee on Small Business Subcommittee on SBA and SBIC Authority, Minority Enterprise and General Small Business Problems, on October 20, 1983, that the SBA's May 3, 1982, proposed notice of rulemaking differed from its March 10, 1980, predecessor in three important ways:

> First, the range of size standards was narrowed to a range of 25 employees to 500 employees. This reflected a widespread view that 15 employees was too low a cutoff while 2,500 employees was too high. Second, SBA proposed a 500-employee ceiling, focusing on smaller firms. Third, SBA responded to sentiments within many procurement-sensitive

---

[69] Ibid., p. 5; and P.L. 96-481, the Small Business Export Expansion Act of 1980.

[70] U.S. Congress, Senate Committee on Small Business, *Small Business Administration's Size Standards*, hearing, 97th Cong., 1st sess., May 5, 1981 (Washington: GPO, 1981), p. 12.

[71] Ibid., p. 11.

industries that the proposed size standards in some cases were too low to accommodate the average procurement currently being performed by small business. Therefore, SBA proposed higher size standards in a number of procurement-sensitive industries, while maintaining the 500-employee cap.[72]

He also testified that the SBA received about 500 comments on the proposed rule, with about 72% of those comments opposing the rule.[73]

Taking those comments into consideration, the SBA reexamined its size standards once again, and, after a year of further consultation with various trade organizations and federal agency procurement officials, issued another notice of proposed rulemaking on May 6, 1983. The 1983 proposal replaced the use of two sets of size standards, one for procurement and another for the SBA's loan and consultative support services, with a single set for all programs; retained most of the size standards that were expressed in terms of average annual sales or receipts; adjusted those size standards for inflation (an upward adjustment of 81%); retained most of the size standards for manufacturing; and made relatively minor changes to the size standards in other industries, with a continued emphasis on a 500-employee ceiling for most industries. The SBA received 630 comments on the proposed rule, with almost 70% supporting it.[74]

SBA Administrator Sanders characterized the SBA's revised size standard proposal as "a fine-tuning of current standards which has the basic support of both the private sector and the Federal agencies that use the basic size standards to achieve their set-aside procurement goals."[75] He also added that "since almost no size standard is proposed to decrease, and most will in fact increase, very few firms will lose their small business status. We estimate that about 39,000 firms will gain small business status."[76] He testified that in percentage terms, in 1983, 97.9% of the nation's 5.2 million firms with employees were classified by the SBA as small. Under the SBA's proposal, 98.6% of all firms with employees would be classified as small.[77] The final rule was published in the *Federal Register* on February 9, 1984.[78]

Representative Parren J. Mitchell, chair of the House Committee on Small Business, expressed disappointment in the SBA's final rule, stating at a congressional oversight hearing on July 30, 1985, that "the government and the business community are still victimized by that same ad hoc, sporadic system that the SBA promised to fix some six years ago."[79] He introduced legislation

---

[72] U.S. Congress, House Committee on Small Business, Subcommittee on SBA and SBIC Authority, Minority Enterprise and General Small Business Problems, Size Standards, hearing, 98th Cong., 1st sess., October 20, 1983 (Washington: GPO, 1983), p. 17. Congress created the Small Business Investment Company (SBIC) program in 1958 to provide small businesses enhanced access to equity capital, long-term loans, and consultative management assistance.

[73] U.S. Congress, House Committee on Small Business, Subcommittee on SBA and SBIC Authority, Minority Enterprise and General Small Business Problems, *H.R. 1178: Small Business Size Standards*, hearing, 99th Cong., 1st sess., July 30, 1985 (Washington: GPO, 1985), p. 198.

[74] U.S. Congress, House Committee on Small Business, Subcommittee on SBA and SBIC Authority, Minority Enterprise and General Small Business Problems, *Size Standards*, hearing, 98th Cong., 1st sess., October 20, 1983 (Washington: GPO, 1983), p. 18.

[75] Ibid.

[76] Ibid.

[77] Ibid.

[78] Ibid.

[79] U.S. Congress, House Committee on Small Business, Subcommittee on SBA and SBIC Authority, Minority Enterprise and General Small Business Problems, *H.R. 1178: Small Business Size Standards*, hearing, 99th Cong., 1st (continued...)

(H.R. 1178, a bill to amend the Small Business Act) that would have required the SBA to adjust its size standard for an industrial classification downward by at least 20% if small business' share of that market equaled or exceeded 60%, and at least 40% of the market share was achieved through the receipt of federal procurement contracts. The bill also mandated a minimum 10% increase in the SBA's size standard for an industrial classification if small business' share of that market was less than 20% and less than 10% of the market share was achieved through the receipt of federal procurement contracts.[80] The bill was opposed by various trade associations, the SBA, and federal agency procurement officials, and was not reported out of committee.[81]

SBA Proposes to Streamline its Size Standards

In 1992, the SBA used 30 different size standards (e.g., 100 or fewer employees, 500 or fewer employees, 1,000 or fewer employees, $5 million in average annual receipts) when classifying firms as small. On December 31, 1992, the SBA issued a notice of proposed rulemaking that was designed "to streamline its size standards by reducing the number of fixed size standard levels to nine."[82] The nine proposed size standards were 100 or fewer, 500 or fewer, 750 or fewer, 1,000 or fewer, or 1,500 or fewer employees; and no more than $5 million, $10 million, $18 million, or $24 million in annual receipts. The annual receipts levels reflected an upward adjustment of 43% for inflation. The SBA argued that the "current system of 30 size standard levels has led to confusion and has created a needless complication of the size standards."[83] The SBA claimed that proposed changes to the size standards would make them more user-friendly for small business owners. It would also restore eligibility to nearly 20,000 firms that were no longer considered small solely because of the effects of inflation. The proposed rule was later withdrawn as a courtesy to allow the incoming Clinton Administration time to review the proposal.[84] The SBA ultimately decided not to pursue this approach because it felt that converting "receipts-based size standards in effect at that time to one of four proposed receipts levels created a number of unacceptable anomalies."[85]

Over the subsequent decade, the SBA reviewed the size standards for some industries on a piecemeal basis and, in 1994, adjusted for inflation its size standards based on firm's annual sales or receipts (an upward adjustment of 48.2%). The SBA estimated that the adjustment would restore eligibility to approximately 20,000 firms that lost small-business status due solely to the effects of inflation.[86]

(...continued)
sess., July 30, 1985 (Washington: GPO, 1985), p. 4.

[80] Ibid., pp. 237-250.

[81] Ibid., pp. 6, 8, 53, 153, 181, 244, 245, 261.

[82] U.S. Small Business Administration, "Small Business Size Standards: Fixed Size Standard Levels," 57 *Federal Register* 62515, December 31, 1992.

[83] Ibid.

[84] U.S. Congress, House Committee on Small Business, Subcommittee on Minority Enterprise, Finance, and Urban Development, *SBA's Efforts to Streamline Size Standards*, hearing, 103rd Cong., 1st sess., May 25, 1993 (Washington: GPO, 1993), pp. 5, 6.

[85] U.S. Small Business Administration, "Small Business Size Standards: Restructuring of Size Standards," 69 *Federal Register* 13130, March 19, 2004.

[86] U.S. Small Business Administration, "Small Business Size Standards: Inflation Adjusted Size Standards," 59 *Federal Register* 16513-16538, April 7, 1994.

In 2002, the SBA adjusted for inflation its annual sales- and receipts-based size standards for the fourth time (an upward adjustment of 15.8%). The SBA estimated that the adjustment would restore eligibility to approximately 8,760 firms that lost small-business status due solely to the effects of inflation. The rule also included a provision that the SBA would assess the impact of inflation on its annual sales- and receipts-based size standards at least once every five years.[87] Then, on March 19, 2004, the SBA, once again, issued a notice of proposed rulemaking in the *Federal Register* to streamline its size standards.[88]

The proposed rule would have established size standards based on the firm's number of employees for all industries, avoiding the need to adjust for inflation size standards based on sales or receipts.[89] At that time, the SBA size standards consisted of 37 different size levels which applied to 1,151 industries and 13 sub-industry activities in the North American Industry Classification System. Thirty size standards were based on annual sales or receipts, five on number of employees (both full- and part-time), one on financial assets, and one on generating capacity. Under the proposed rule, the SBA would use 10 size standards, 5 new employee size standards (adding 50 or fewer, 150 or fewer, 200 or fewer, 300 or fewer, and 400 or fewer employees), and the existing 5 employee size standards (100 or fewer, 500 or fewer, 750 or fewer, 1,000 or fewer, and 1,500 or fewer employees).[90]

The proposed rule would not have changed any of the size standards that were already based on number of employees. It would have converted size standards based on receipts, sales, assets, or generating capacity to an employee-based size standard. The SBA argued that the use of a single size standard would "help to simplify size standards" and "tends to be a more stable measure of business size" than other measures.[91] It added that the proposed rule would change 514 size standards and that, after the proposed conversion to the use of number of employees, of the "approximately 4.4 million businesses in the industries with revised size standards, 35,200 businesses could gain and 34,100 could lose small business eligibility, with the net effect of 1,100 additional businesses defined as small."[92]

The SBA received more than 4,500 comments on the proposed rule, with a majority (51%) supporting the rule, but with "a large number of comments opposing various aspects of SBA's approach to simplifying size standards."[93] In addition, Representative Donald Manzullo, chair of the House Committee on Small Business, and Senator Olympia Snowe, chair of the Senate Committee on Small Business and Entrepreneurship, opposed the proposed rule.[94] Senator John

---

[87] U.S. Small Business Administration, "Small Business Size Standards: Inflation Adjustment to Size Standards," 67 *Federal Register* 65285-65290, October 24, 2002.

[88] U.S. Small Business Administration, "Small Business Size Standards: Restructuring of Size Standards," 69 *Federal Register* 13129-13164, March 19, 2004.

[89] Ibid.

[90] Ibid., p. 13130.

[91] Ibid., pp. 13131-13132.

[92] Ibid., p. 13138.

[93] U.S. Small Business Administration, "Small Business Size Standards: Selected Size Standards Issues," 69 *Federal Register* 70197, December 3, 2004; and U.S. Small Business Administration, "Small Business Size Standards: Selected Size Standards Issues," 70 *Federal Register* 2976, January 19, 2005.

[94] Representative Donald A. Manzullo and Representative Nydia M. Velázquez, "Small Business Size Standards; Restructuring of Size Standards, 69 *Federal Register* 13,130 (March 19, 2004); Letter to Gary M. Jackson, SBA Assistant Administrator for Size Standards," July 8, 2004, at http://democrats.smallbusiness.house.gov/Size%20Standards%20Comment%20Letter%200704.pdf; and U.S. Newswire, "Snowe Hails SBA's Withdrawal of (continued...)

Kerry, ranking minority Member of the Senate Committee on Small Business and Entrepreneurship, sent a letter to the SBA requesting that it "rescind its proposal to restructure the way companies are determined to be small businesses" because "small business advocates have informed me that this proposal could threaten or eliminate over 8 million jobs" and "the proposal would punish the 34,000 firms that are currently considered small, have been acting in good faith with the Federal government, but will lose their small business status abruptly as a result of the change."[95] The SBA withdrew the proposed rule on July 1, 2004. Senator Snowe was quoted in a press interview later that day that she supported the SBA's decision to rescind the proposed rule:

> At the eleventh hour, the SBA has corrected its course and averted costly disruptions for small businesses across the country.... The SBA's proposed rule would have sent a tidal wave crashing over small business, effectively wiping out the foundation on which countless firms currently operate. Small firms still recovering from last year's slow economy are in no shape to cope with such a sea change in the regulatory landscape.[96]

Senator Snowe reportedly urged the SBA to proceed cautiously with any future effort to restructure its size standards, emphasizing that any such effort should include a thorough dialogue with business owners and Congress.[97]

In 2005, the SBA adjusted for inflation size standards based on firms' annual sales or receipts (an upward adjustment of 8.7%). The SBA estimated that the adjustment restored eligibility to approximately 12,000 firms that lost small-business status due solely to the effects of inflation. In 2008, the SBA made another adjustment for inflation to its annual sales- and receipts-based standards (another upward adjustment of 8.7%). The SBA estimated that the adjustment restored eligibility for approximately 10,400 firms that lost small-business status due solely to the effects of inflation.[98]

SBA Adopts a More Incremental, Targeted Approach

In June 2008, the SBA announced that it would undertake a comprehensive, two-year review of its size standards, proceeding one industrial sector at a time, starting with Retail Trade (NAICS Sector 44-45), Accommodations and Food Services (NAICS Sector 72), and Other Services

---

(...continued)

New Size Standards Proposal; Decision Spares Small Firms Costly Disruptions," July 1, 2004, p. 1, at http://proquest.umi.com/pqdweb?did=657675071&sid=1&Fmt=3&clientId=45714&RQT=309&VName=PQD.

[95] U.S. Senate Committee on Small Business and Entrepreneurship, "Kerry Urges SBA to Withdraw Small Business Size Standard Proposal," press release, June 29, 2004, at http://sbc.senate.gov/press/record.cfm?id=223511.

[96] U.S. Newswire, "Snowe Hails SBA's Withdrawal of New Size Standards Proposal; Decision Spares Small Firms Costly Disruptions," July 1, 2004, p. 1, at http://proquest.umi.com/pqdweb?did=657675071&sid=1&Fmt=3&clientId=45714&RQT=309&VName=PQD.

[97] Ibid.

[98] U.S. Small Business Administration, "Small Business Size Standards, Inflation Adjustment to Size Standards; Business Loan Program; Disaster Assistance Loan Program," 70 *Federal Register* 72577, December 6, 2005; and U.S. Small Business Administration, "Small Business Size Standards: Inflation Adjustment to Size Standards; Business Loan Program, and Disaster Assistance Loan Program," 73 *Federal Register* 41237-41254, July 18, 2008.

(NAICS Sector 81).[99] The SBA argued that it was concerned that "not all of its size standards may now adequately define small businesses in the U.S. economy, which has seen industry consolidations, technological advances, emerging new industries, shifting societal preferences, and other significant industrial changes."[100] It added that its reliance on an ad hoc approach "to scrutinizing the limited number of specific industries during a year, while worthwhile, leaves unexamined many deserving industries for updating and may create over time a set of illogical size standards."[101]

The SBA announced that it would begin its analysis of its size standards by assuming that "$6.5 million [now $7.0 million] is an appropriate size standard for those industries with receipts size standards and 500 employees for those industries with employee size standards."[102] It would then analyze the following industry characteristics: "average firm size; average asset size (a proxy for startup costs); competition, as measured by the market share of the four largest firms in the industry; and, the distribution of market share by firm size—that is, are firms in the industry generally very small firms, or dominated by very large firms."[103] Then, before making its final determination on the size standard, it would "examine the participation of small businesses in federal contracting and SBA's guaranteed loan program at the current size standard level. Depending on the level of small business participation, additional consideration may be given to the level of the current size standard and the analysis of industry factors."[104]

The SBA later announced in its Semiannual Regulatory Agenda, published on November 24, 2008, that it planned to issue a notice of proposed rulemaking concerning size standards for Retail Trade (NAICS Sector 44-45), Accommodations and Food Services (NAICS Sector 72), and Other Services (NAICS Sector 81) in January 2009.[105] The SBA issued the notices for those industries on October 21, 2009.[106]

In April 2009, the SBA announced that it was going to simplify the administration and use of its size standards by reducing the number of receipt based size standards it used when establishing or approving a size standard:

> For many years, SBA has been concerned about the complexity of determining small business status caused by a large number of varying receipts based size standards (see 69 FR

---

[99] U.S. Small Business Administration, "Small Business Size Standards: Public Meetings on a Comprehensive Review of Small Business Size Standards," 73 *Federal Register* 30440 - 30442, May 27, 2008. Other Services (NAICS Sector 81) include repair and maintenance, personal and laundry services, and religious, grantmaking, civic, professional, and similar organizations.

[100] U.S. Small Business Administration, "Small Business Size Standards: Public Meetings on a Comprehensive Review of Small Business Size Standards," 73 *Federal Register* 30441, May 27, 2008.

[101] Ibid.

[102] U.S. Small Business Administration, "Size Standards Comprehensive Review," June 3, 2008, at http://archive.sba.gov/idc/groups/public/documents/adacct/june_3_public_presentation_rem.pdf.

[103] Ibid.

[104] Ibid.

[105] U.S. Small Business Administration, "Small Business Administration Semiannual Regulatory Agenda," 73 *Federal Register* 71449, 71450, November 24, 2008.

[106] U.S. Small Business Administration, "Small Business Size Standards: Retail Trade," 74 *Federal Register* 53924-53940, October 21, 2009; U.S. Small Business Administration, "Small Business Size Standards: Accommodation and Food Services Industries," 74 *Federal Register* 53913-53924, October 21, 2009; and U.S. Small Business Administration, "Small Business Size Standards: Other Services Industries," 74 *Federal Register* 53941-53954, October 21, 2009.

13130 (March 4, 2004) and 57 FR 62515 (December 31, 1992)). At the start of current comprehensive size standards review, there were 31 different levels of receipts based size standards. They ranged from $0.75 million to $35.5 million, and many of them applied to one or only a few industries. The SBA believes that to have so many different size standards with small variations among them is unnecessary and difficult to justify analytically. To simplify managing and using size standards, SBA proposes that there be fewer size standard levels. This will produce more common size standards for businesses operating in related industries. This will also result in greater consistency among the size standards for industries that have similar economic characteristics.

Under the current comprehensive size standards review, SBA is proposing to establish eight "fixed-level" receipts based size standards: $5.0 million, $7.0 million, $10.0 million, $14.0 million, $19.0 million, $25.5 million, $30.0 million, and $35.5 million. These levels are established by taking into consideration the minimum, maximum and the most commonly used current receipts based size standards.[107]

The SBA also announced that "to simplify size standards further" it "may propose a common size standard for closely related industries."[108] The SBA argued

> although the size standard analysis may support a separate size standard for each industry, SBA believes that establishing different size standards for closely related industries may not always be appropriate. For example, in cases where many of the same businesses operate in the same multiple industries, a common size standard for those industries might better reflect the Federal marketplace. This might also make size standards among related industries more consistent than separate size standards for each of those industries.[109]

Table 2 shows the eight fixed levels for receipts-based size standards and the eight fixed levels for its employee-based size standards that the SBA is currently applying when establishing or reviewing size standards under its ongoing review of its size standards.

Table 2. Industry-Based Size Standard Levels Currently Being Applied During the SBA's On-going Review of its Size Standards

Receipts-Based Levels	Employee-Based Levels
$5.0 million	50 employees
$7.0 million (anchor)	100 employees (wholesale anchor)
$10.0 million	150 employees
$14.0 million	200 employees
$19.0 million	250 employees
$25.5 million	500 employees (manufacturing anchor)
$30.0 million	750 employees
$35.5 million	1,000 employees

---

[107] U.S. Small Business Administration, "Small Business Size Standards Methodology," April 2009, pp. 21, 22, at http://www.sba.gov/sites/default/files/size_standards_methodology.pdf.
[108] Ibid., pp. 22- 23.
[109] Ibid., p. 23.

Source: U.S. Small Business Administration, "Small Business Size Standards Methodology," April 2009, pp. 21-23, at http://www.sba.gov/sites/default/files/size_standards_methodology.pdf.

Notes: At the start of the current comprehensive size standards review which began in 2008, the SBA had 41 different size standards: number of employees (7 size standards), average annual receipts in the previous three years (31 size standards), average assets (1 size standard), annual megawatt hours of electric output in the preceding fiscal year (1 size standard), and a combination of number of employees and barrel per day refining capacity (1 size standard). It also currently has 11 other size standards for its financial and other programs.

The final rules for Retail Trade (NAICS Sector 44-45), Accommodations and Food Services (NAICS Sector 72), and Other Services (NAICS Sector 81) were published in the *Federal Register* on October 6, 2010, with an effective date of November 5, 2010.[110] The SBA increased size standards for 46 of the 76 industries in Retail Trade (NAICS Sector 44-45), 5 of the 15 industries in Accommodations and Food Services (NAICS Sector 72), and 18 of the 47 industries in Other Services (NAICS Sector 81).[111] The SBA's analysis supported a decrease to the current size standards for 23 industries in Retail Trade (NAICS Sector 44-45), 7 industries in Accommodations and Food Services (NAICS Sector 72), and 20 industries in Other Services (NAICS Sector 81). However, the SBA retained those size standards because "proposing to lower small business size standards would be inconsistent with its on-going effort to promote small business assistance under the Recovery Act."[112] The SBA has continued the practice of retaining size standards when the SBA's economic analysis supports a decrease because "lowering small business size standards is not in the best interest of small businesses in the current economic environment" and would "run counter to what SBA and the federal government are doing to help small businesses and create jobs."[113]

On April 26, 2010, the SBA announced that it planned to issue final size standard rules for Professional, Scientific and Technical Services (NAICS Sector 54) and Transportation and Warehousing (NAICS Sector 48-49) in August 2010.[114] The SBA published a notice of proposed rulemaking in the *Federal Register* concerning size standards Professional, Scientific and Technical Services (NAICS Sector 54) on March 16, 2011,[115] and Transportation and

---

[110] U.S. Small Business Administration, "Small Business Size Standards: Retail Trade," 75 *Federal Register* 61597-61604, October 6, 2010; U.S. Small Business Administration, "Small Business Size Standards: Accommodations and Food Service Industries," 75 *Federal Register* 61604-61609, October 6, 2010; and U.S. Small Business Administration, "Small Business Size Standards: Other Services," 75 *Federal Register* 61591-61596, October 6, 2010. The final rule for the retail trade industries also converted the measure of size for new car dealers from annual receipts to number of employees.

[111] Ibid.

[112] U.S. Small Business Administration, "Small Business Size Standards: Retail Trade," 75 *Federal Register* 61598, October 6, 2010; U.S. Small Business Administration, "Small Business Size Standards: Accommodations and Food Service Industries," 75 *Federal Register* 61605, October 6, 2010; and U.S. Small Business Administration, "Small Business Size Standards: Other Services," 75 *Federal Register* 61592, October 6, 2010.

[113] U.S. Small Business Administration, "Small Business Size Standards: Agriculture, Forestry, Fishing, and Hunting," 77 *Federal Register* 55763, September 11, 2012.

[114] U.S. Small Business Administration, "Small Business Size Standards: Retail Trade," 75 *Federal Register* 21895, April 26, 2010; U.S. Small Business Administration, "Small Business Size Standards: Accommodations and Food Service Industries," 75 *Federal Register* 21895, April 26, 2010; U.S. Small Business Administration, "Small Business Size Standards: Other Services," 75 *Federal Register* 21895, April 26, 2010; U.S. Small Business Administration, "Small Business Size Standards: Professional Scientific and Technical Services," 75 *Federal Register* 21893, April 26, 2010; and U.S. Small Business Administration, "Small Business Size Standards: Transportation and Warehousing Industries," 75 *Federal Register* 21894, April 26, 2010.

[115] The proposed rule would have increased small business size standards for 35 industries and one sub-industry within the professional, scientific and technical services industries. The SBA estimated that about 9,450 additional firms would obtain small business status if the proposed rule became effective and the small business share of total industry (continued...)

Warehousing (NAICS Sector 48-49) on May 13, 2011.[116] The SBA issued the final size standard rule for Professional, Scientific and Technical Services (NAICS Sector 54) on February 10, 2012.[117] It issued the final size standard rule for Transportation and Warehousing (NAICS Sector 48-49) on February 24, 2012.[118]

Congress Requires Periodic Size Standard Reviews

As mentioned previously, P.L. 111-240, the Small Business Jobs Act of 2010, requires the SBA to conduct a detailed review of not less than one-third of the SBA's industry size standards during the 18-month period beginning on the date of enactment (September 27, 2010) and during every 18-month period thereafter.[119] The act directs the SBA to "make appropriate adjustments to the size standards" to reflect market conditions, and to report to the House Committee on Small Business and the Senate Committee on Small Business and Entrepreneurship and make publicly available "not later than 30 days" after the completion of each review information regarding the factors evaluated as part of each review, the criteria used for any revised size standard, and why the SBA did, or did not, adjust each size standard that was reviewed. The act also requires the SBA to ensure that each industry size standard is reviewed at least once every five years.[120]

On July 7, 2011, the SBA announced as part of its "comprehensive review of all small business size standards" that it was evaluating the size standards in six NAICS Sectors as follows:

- Utilities (NAICS Sector 22);
- Information (NAICS Sector 51);
- Administrative and Support, Waste Management and Remediation Services (NAICS Sector 56);

(...continued)
receipts in those industries would increase from about 35% under the current size standards to 41%. The number of firms that would obtain eligibility under the proposed rule represents about 1.2% of the total number of firms in those industries defined as small under current standards. Also, the SBA's analysis supported a decrease in the size standards in 14 industries and one sub-industry, but the SBA concluded that "lowering small business size standards is not in the best interests of small businesses under current economic conditions." See U.S. Small Business Administration, "Small Business Size Standards: Professional, Scientific and Technical Services," 76 *Federal Register* 14323-14341, March 16, 2011.

[116] The proposed rule would have increased small business size standards for 22 industries within the transportation and warehousing industries. The SBA estimated that about 1,200 additional firms would obtain small business status if the proposed rule became effective and the small business share of total industry receipts in those industries would increase from about 36% under the current size standards to 39%. The number of firms that would obtain eligibility under the proposed rule represents about 0.7% of the total number of firms in those industries defined as small under current standards. Also, the SBA's analysis supported a decrease in the size standards in 18 industries, but the SBA concluded that "lowering small business size standards is not in the best interests of small businesses under current economic conditions." See U.S. Small Business Administration, "Small Business Size Standards: Transportation and Warehousing," 76 *Federal Register* 27935-27952, May 13, 2011.

[117] U.S. Small Business Administration, "Small Business Size Standards: Professional, Technical, and Scientific Services," 77 *Federal Register* 7490-7515, February 10, 2012.

[118] U.S. Small Business Administration, "Small Business Size Standards: Transportation and Warehousing," 77 *Federal Register* 10943-10950, February 24, 2012.

[119] P.L. 111-240, the Small Business Act of 2010, §1344. Updated Size Standards.

[120] Ibid.

- Real Estate Rental and Leasing (NAICS Sector 53);
- Educational Services (NAICS Sector 61); and
- Health Care and Social Assistance Services (NAICS Sector 62).[121]

The SBA also announced that once these reviews are complete that it anticipates reviewing size standards in the following NAICS Sectors in this sequence:

- Arts, Entertainment, and Recreation (NAICS Sector 71);
- Construction (NAICS Sector 23);
- Wholesale Trade (NAICS Sector 42);
- Finance and Insurance (NAICS Sector 52);
- Management of Companies (NAICS Sector 55);
- Mining (NAICS Sector 21);
- Agriculture, Forestry, Fishing and Hunting (NAICS Sector 11); and
- Manufacturing (NAICS Sector 31-33).[122]

Table 3 provides the status of SBA industry size standard reviews since 2010. The table includes

- the date the SBA published or anticipates to publish in the *Federal Register* a notice of intent to review the size standard;
- the date the SBA published or anticipates to publish in the *Federal Register* a notice of proposed rulemaking for the size standard;
- the recommended change proposed in the notice of proposed rulemaking;
- the date the SBA published or anticipates to publish in the *Federal Register* the final rule for the size standard; and
- the change that took place as a result of the final rule.

---

[121] U.S. Small Business Administration, "Semiannual Regulatory Agenda," 76 *Federal Register* 40140-40142, July 7, 2011.

[122] U.S. Small Business Administration, Office of Congressional and Legislative Affairs, "Correspondence with the author," March 30, 2012.

Table 3. Status of SBA Size Standard Reviews, 2010-2013

NAICS Sectors	Notice of Intent to Review the Standard	Notice of Proposed Rulemaking	Recommended Change	Final Rule	Final Change
Transportation and Warehousing (NAICS Sector 48-49)	75 *Federal Register* 21894, Apr. 26, 2010	76 *Federal Register* 27935-27952, May 13, 2011	Would increase size standards for 22 industries	77 *Federal Register* 10943-10950, Feb. 24, 2012 (effective Mar. 26, 2012)	Increased size standards for 22 industries
Professional, Scientific and Technical Services (NAICS Sector 54)	75 *Federal Register* 21893, 21894 Apr. 26, 2010	76 *Federal Register* 14323-14341, Mar. 16, 2011	Would increase size standards for 35 industries and 1 sub-industry	77 *Federal Register* 7488-7515, Feb. 10, 2012 (effective Mar. 12, 2012)	Increased size standards for 34 industries and 3 sub-industries[a]
Information (NAICS Sector 51)	76 *Federal Register* 40140-40142, July 7, 2011	76 *Federal Register* 63216-63229, Oct. 12, 2011	Would increase size standards for 15 industries	77 *Federal Register* 72702-72709, Dec. 6, 2012 (effective Jan. 7, 2013)	Increased size standards for 15 industries
Administrative and Support, Waste Management and Remediation Services (NAICS Sector 56)	76 *Federal Register* 40140-40142, July 7, 2011	76 *Federal Register* 63510-63525, Oct. 12, 2011	Would increase size standards for 37 industries	77 *Federal Register* 72691-72702, Dec. 6, 2012 (effective Jan. 7, 2013)	Increased size standards for 37 industries
Educational Services (NAICS Sector 61)	76 *Federal Register* 40140-40142, July 7, 2011	76 *Federal Register* 70667-70680, Nov. 15, 2011	Would increase size standards for nine industries	77 *Federal Register* 58739-58747, September 24, 2012 (effective Oct. 24, 2012)	Increased size standards for nine industries

NAICS Sectors	Notice of Intent to Review the Standard	Notice of Proposed Rulemaking	Recommended Change	Final Rule	Final Change
Real Estate, Rental and Leasing (NAICS Sector 53)	76 *Federal Register* 40140-40142, July 7, 2011	76 *Federal Register* 70680-70694, Nov.15, 2011	Would increase size standards for 20 industries and 1 sub-industry	77 *Federal Register* 58747-58755, September 24, 2012 (effective Oct. 24, 2012)	Increased size standards for 21 industries and 1 sub-industry
Health Care and Social Assistance Services (NAICS Sector 62)	76 *Federal Register* 40140-40142, July 7, 2011	77 *Federal Register* 11001-11017, Feb. 24, 2012	Would increase size standards for 28 industries	77 *Federal Register* 58755-58761, September 24, 2012 (effective Oct. 24, 2012)	Increased size standards for 28 industries
Arts, Entertainment, and Recreation (NAICS Sector 71)	77 *Federal Register* 8024, February 13, 2012	77 *Federal Register* 42211-42225, July 18, 2012	Would increase size standards for 17 industries	78 *Federal Register* 37417-37422, June 20, 2013 (effective July 22, 2013)	Increased size standards for 17 industries
Construction (NAICS Sector 23)	77 *Federal Register* 8024, February 13, 2012	77 *Federal Register* 42197-42211, July 18, 2012	Would increase size standards for one industry and one sub-industry	78 *Federal Register* 77334-77343, Dec. 23, 2013 (effective Jan. 22, 2014)	Increased size standards for one industry and one sub-industry

NAICS Sectors	Notice of Intent to Review the Standard	Notice of Proposed Rulemaking	Recommended Change	Final Rule	Final Change
Utilities (NAICS Sector 22)	76 Federal Register 40140-40142, July 7, 2011	77 Federal Register 42441-42454, July 19, 2012	Would increase size standards for three industries and convert six industries from no more than 4 million megawatt hours in electric output in the preceding fiscal year to no more than 500 employees	78 Federal Register 77343-77351, Dec. 23, 2013 (effective Jan. 22, 2014)	Increased size standards for three industries and converted 10 industries from no more than 4 million megawatt hours in electric output in the preceding fiscal year to number of employees (varying by industry)
Finance and Insurance (NAICS Sector 52)	NA	77 Federal Register 55737-55755, September, 11, 2012	Would increase size standards for 37 industries and change the measure of size from total assets to annual receipts for 1 industry	78 Federal Register 37409-37417, June 20, 2013 (effective July 22, 2013)	Increased size standards for 36 industries, and changed the measure of size from total assets to annual receipts for 1 industry
Management of Companies (NAICS Sector 55)	NA	77 Federal Register 55737-55755, September, 11, 2012	Would increase size standards for two industries	78 Federal Register 37409-37417, June 20, 2013 (effective July 22, 2013)	Increased size standards for two industries

NAICS Sectors	Notice of Intent to Review the Standard	Notice of Proposed Rulemaking	Recommended Change	Final Rule	Final Change
Agriculture, Forestry, Fishing and Hunting (NAICS Sector 11)	NA	77 Federal Register 55755-55768, September, 11, 2012	Would increase size standards for 11 industries	78 Federal Register 37398-37404, June 20, 2013 (effective July 22, 2013)	Increased size standards for 11 industries
Support Activities for Mining (within NAICS Sector 21)	NA	77 Federal Register 72766, December, 6, 2012	Would increase size standards for three industries	78 Federal Register 37404-37408, June 20, 2013 (effective July 22, 2013)	Increased size standards for three industries
Mining, Quarrying, and Oil and Gas Extraction (NAICS Sector 21)	78 Federal Register 1639, Jan. 8, 2013	cites 77 Federal Register 72766, December, 6, 2012	Expected in 2014	Expected in 2014	Expected in 2014
Wholesale Trade (NAICS Sector 42)	78 Federal Register 1639, Jan. 8, 2013	Was expected in March 2013	Expected in 2014	Expected in 2014	Expected in 2014
Manufacturing (NAICS Sector 31-33)	78 Federal Register 1639, Jan. 8, 2013	Was expected in March 2013	Expected in 2014	Expected in 2014	Expected in 2014
Other Industries with Employee-Based Size Standards not Part of Manufacturing or Wholesale Trade (primarily within NAICS Sectors 51 and 54)	78 Federal Register 1639, Jan. 8, 2013	Was expected in March 2013	Expected in 2014	Expected in 2014	Expected in 2014

Source: *Federal Register* as cited in the table.

a. Also increased one size standard (Computer and Office Machine Repair and Maintenance) in NAICS Sector 81, Other Services, that was not reviewed during the SBA's review of that sector in 2010.

SBA's Definitions for Small Business

The SBA, relying on statutory language, defines a small business as a concern that is organized for profit; has a place of business in the United States; operates primarily within the United States or makes a significant contribution to the economy through payment of taxes or use of American products, materials, or labor; is independently owned and operated; and is not dominant in its field on a national basis. The business may be a sole proprietorship, partnership, corporation, or any other legal form.[123]

The SBA uses two measures to determine if a business is small: industry specific size standards or a combination of the business's net worth and net income. For example, the SBA's Small Business Investment Company (SBIC) program allows businesses to qualify as small if they meet the SBA's size standard for the industry in which the applicant is primarily engaged, or an alternative net worth and net income based size standard which has been established for the SBIC program. The SBIC's alternative size standard is currently set as a maximum net worth of not more than $18 million and average after-tax net income for the preceding two years of not more than $6 million.[124] All of the company's subsidiaries, parent companies, and affiliates are considered in determining if it meets the size standard. The SBA decided to apply the net worth and net income measures to the SBIC program "because investment companies evaluate businesses using these measures to decide whether or not to make an investment in them."[125]

Businesses participating in the SBA's 504/Certified Development Company (504/CDC) loan guaranty program are to be deemed small if they did not have a tangible net worth in excess of $8.5 million and did not have an average net income in excess of $3 million after taxes for the preceding two years.[126] As discussed below, P.L. 111-240, the Small Business Jobs Act of 2010, increased these threshold amounts on an interim basis to not more than $15 million in tangible net worth and not more than $5 million in average net income after federal taxes for the two full fiscal years before the date of the application. All of the company's subsidiaries, parent companies, and affiliates are considered in determining if it meets the size standard. Also, before May 5, 2009, businesses participating in the SBA's 7(a) loan guaranty program, including its express programs, were deemed small if they met the SBA's size standards for firms in the industries described in the North American Industry Classification System (NAICS).[127]

Alternative Size Standards

Using authority provided under P.L. 111-5, the American Recovery and Reinvestment Act of 2009, the SBA temporarily applied the 504/CDC program's size standards as an alternative for 7(a) loans approved from May 5, 2009, through September 30, 2010.[128] Firms applying for a 7(a)

---

[123] 13 CFR §121.105. Affiliations between businesses, or relationships allowing one party control or the power of control over another, generally count in size determinations. Businesses can thus be determined to be other than small because of their involvement in joint ventures, subcontracting arrangements, or franchise or license agreements, among other things, provided that their personnel numbers or income, plus those of their affiliate(s), are over the pertinent size threshold. 13 CFR §121.103. For further analysis, see CRS Report R40744, *The "8(a) Program" for Small Businesses Owned and Controlled by the Socially and Economically Disadvantaged: Legal Requirements and Issues*, by Kate M. Manuel.

[124] 13 CFR §107.700; 13 CFR §107.710; 13 CFR §301(c)(2); and 13 CFR §301(c)(1).

[125] U.S. Small Business Administration, Office of Government Contracting and Business Development, "SBA Size Standards Methodology," April 2009, p. 8, at http://www.sba.gov/sites/default/files/size_standards_methodology.pdf.

[126] U.S. Small Business Administration, "SOP 50 10 5(C): Lender and Development Company Loan Programs," (effective October 1, 2010), p. 266, at http://www.sba.gov/sites/default/files/serv_sops_50105c_loan_0.pdf; and U.S. Small Business Administration, "SOP 50 10 5(E): Lender and Development Company Loan Programs," (effective June 1, 2012), p. 92, at http://www.sba.gov/sites/default/files/SOP%2050%2010%205(E)%20(6-27-2013)%20change%20of%20ownership%20eff%20date%207-1-13%20clean.pdf.

[127] 13 CFR §121.201.

[128] U.S. Small Business Administration, "Small Business Size Standards; Temporary Alternative Size Standards for (continued...)

loan during that time period qualified as small using either the SBA's industry size standards or the 504/CDC program's size standard. The provision's intent was to enhance the ability of small businesses to access the capital necessary to create and retain jobs during the economic recovery.

P.L. 111-240 made the use of alternative size standards for the 7(a) program permanent. The act directs the SBA to establish an alternative size standard for both the 7(a) and 504/CDC programs that uses maximum tangible net worth and average net income as an alternative to the use of industry standards. The act also establishes, until the date on which the alternative size standard is established, an interim alternative size standard for the 7(a) and 504/CDC programs of not more than $15 million in tangible net worth and not more than $5 million in average net income after federal taxes (excluding any carry-over losses) for the two full fiscal years before the date of the application.[129]

Industry Size Standards

The SBA administrator has the authority to establish and modify size standards for particular industries. At the start of the current review of comprehensive size standards which started in 2008, the SBA had 41 different size standards: number of employees (7 size standards, 8 slightly different ones under the new methodology); average annual receipts in the previous three years (31 size standards, 8 under the new methodology); average assets (1 size standard); annual megawatt hours of electric output in the preceding fiscal year (1 size standard); and a combination of number of employees and barrel per day refining capacity (1 size standard).[130] Overall, the SBA currently classifies about 97% of all employer firms as small.[131] These firms account for about 30% of industry receipts.

(...continued)
7(a) Business Loan Program," 74 *Federal Register* 20577, May 5, 2009.

[129] P.L. 111-240, the Small Business Act of 2010, §1116. Alternative Size Standards. S. 3103, the Small Business Job Creation Act of 2010, introduced by then-Senator Olympia Snowe on March 10, 2010, and referred to the Senate Committee on Finance, and S. 2869, the Small Business Job Creation and Access to Capital Act of 2009, introduced by Senator Mary Landrieu on December 10, 2009, and reported favorably by the Senate Committee on Small Business and Entrepreneurship, would have authorized the SBA to establish an alternative size standard for the SBA's 7(a) and 504/CDC loan programs. Both bills would have used maximum tangible net worth of not more than $15 million and average net income after federal taxes of not more than $5 million for the two full fiscal years before the date of the application as an alternative to the use of the SBA's industry size standards. Senator Snowe stated on the Senate floor, on December 10, 2009, that the proposed alternative size standard in S. 2869 would "help more small businesses meet the SBA's requirements to access SBA-backed loans." Senator Olympia Snowe, "Statements on Introduced Bills and Joint Resolutions," remarks in the Senate, *Congressional Record*, daily edition, vol. 155, no. 185 (December 10, 2009), p. S12913.

[130] 13 CFR §121.102; 13 CFR §121.104; 13 CFR §121.106; and 13 CFR §121.201. Almost all industries have only one measure of size. A few industries use a combination of measures. For example, the petroleum refinery industry uses a combination of refining capacity and number of employees. Also, the number of employees of a concern is its average number of persons employed for each pay period over the concern's latest 12 months. Any person on the payroll must be included as one employee regardless of hours worked or temporary status. Also, if a concern has not been in business for three years, the average weekly revenue for the number of weeks the concern has been in business is multiplied by 52 to determine its average annual receipts.

[131] U.S. Small Business Administration, "SBA's Size Standards Analysis: An Overview on Methodology and Comprehensive Size Standards Review," power point presentation, Khem R. Sharma, SBA Office of Size Standards, July 13, 2011, p. 4, at http://www.actgov.org/sigcom/SIGs/SIGs/SBSIG/Documents/2011%20-%20Documents%20and%20Presentations/Size%20Stds%20Presentation_SIG%20Meeting.pdf.

The SBA generally "prefers to use average annual receipts as a size measure because it measures the value of output of a business and can be easily verified by business tax returns and financial records."[132] However, historically, the SBA has used the number of employees to determine if manufacturing and mining companies are small. As a starting point, the SBA

> presumes $7.0 million as an appropriate size standard for the services, retail trade, construction, and other industries with receipts based size standards; 500 employees for the manufacturing, mining and other industries with employee based size standards; and 100 employees for the wholesale trade industries. These three levels, referred to as "anchor size standards," are not minimum size standards, but rather benchmarks or starting points. To the extent an industry displays "differing industry characteristics," a size standard higher, or in some cases lower, than an anchor size standard is supportable.[133]

Before a proposed change to the size standards can take effect, the SBA's Office of Size Standards (OSS) undertakes an analysis of the change's likely impact on the affected industry, focusing on the industry's overall degree of competition and the competitiveness of the firms within the industry. The analysis includes an assessment of the following five industry factors: average firm size, degree of competition within the industry, start-up costs and entry barriers, distribution of firms by size, and small business share in federal contracts.[134] The SBA also considers several other secondary factors "as they are relevant to the industries and the interests of small businesses, including technological change, competition among industries, industry growth trends, and impacts on SBA programs."[135]

Any changes to size standards must follow the rulemaking procedures of the Administrative Procedure Act. A proposed rule changing a size standard is first published in the *Federal Register*, allowing for public comment. It must include documentation establishing that a significant problem exists that requires a revision of the size standard, plus an economic analysis of the change. Comments from the public, plus any other new information, are reviewed and evaluated before a final rule is promulgated establishing a new size standard.

The SBA uses employment size to determine eligibility for 509 industries, including all 364 manufacturing industries, 25 of 29 mining industries, and all 71 wholesale trade industries. Most manufacturing industries (247 of 364 classifications, or 67.9%) have an upper limit of 500 employees; some have an upper limit of 750 employees (53 of 364 classifications, or 14.6%); some have an upper limit of 1,000 employees (61 of 364 classifications, or 16.8%); and 3 (ammunition, except small arms, manufacturers, petroleum refineries, and aircraft manufacturers) have an upper limit of 1,500 employees.[136] All 25 of the mining industries that use employment to

---

[132] U.S. Small Business Administration, Office of Government Contracting and Business Development, "SBA Size Standards Methodology," April 2009, p. 8, at http://www.sba.gov/sites/default/files/size_standards_methodology.pdf.

[133] Ibid., p. 1. SBA established 500 employees as the anchor size standard for the manufacturing industries at SBA's inception in 1953, and shortly thereafter established a receipts based anchor size standard of $1 million in average annual receipts for the nonmanufacturing industries. The receipts based anchor size standard has been adjusted periodically for inflation.

[134] 13 C.F.R. §121.102.

[135] U.S. Small Business Administration, Office of Government Contracting and Business Development, "SBA Size Standards Methodology," April 2009, p. 1, at http://www.sba.gov/sites/default/files/size_standards_methodology.pdf.

[136] U.S. Small Business Administration, "Table of Small Business Size Standards," July 22, 2013, at http://www.sba.gov/content/table-small-business-size-standards.

determine eligibility have an upper limit of 500 employees. All 71 of the wholesale trades industries have an upper limit of 100 employees.[137]

The SBA currently has eight different employee-based size standards (50 or fewer, 100 or fewer, 150 or fewer, 200 or fewer, 500 or fewer, 750 or fewer, 1,000 or fewer, and 1,500 or fewer employees) in 509 industries.[138] Under the new methodology, the SBA will use the following eight slightly different employee-based size standards when establishing new, or reviewing existing, size standards: 50 or fewer, 100 or fewer, 150 or fewer, 200 or fewer, 250 or fewer, 500 or fewer, 750 or fewer, and 1,000 or fewer.

The SBA uses average annual receipts over the three most recently completed fiscal years to determine program eligibility for most other industries (533 of 1,047 industries, or 50.9%).[139] The SBA also uses average asset size as reported in the firm's four quarterly financial statements for the preceding year to determine eligibility for five finance industries, and a combination of number of employees and barrel per day refining capacity for petroleum refineries.[140]

As mentioned previously, at the start of the current comprehensive size standards review which began in 2008, the SBA had 31 different size limits using the firm's average annual sales or receipts, ranging from no more than $0.75 million to no more than $35.5 million, to determine program eligibility in 538 industries. In some instances, there is considerable variation in the size standards used within each industrial sector. For example, the SBA uses 10 different size standards to determine eligibility for 69 industries in the retail trade sector.[141] In general

- most administrative and support service industries have an upper limit of either $14.0 million or $19.0 million in average annual sales or receipts;
- most agricultural industries have an upper limit of $0.75 million in average annual sales or receipts;[142]
- most construction of buildings and civil engineering construction industries have an upper limit of $33.5 million in average annual sales or receipts, and most construction specialty trade contractors have an upper limit of $14.0 million in average annual sales or receipts;
- most educational services industries have an upper limit of either $7.0 million or $10 million in average annual sales or receipts;

---

[137] Ibid. Since 1986, all industries in the Wholesale Trade Sector have had the 100-employee size standard. For procurement purposes, the SBA's size standard is 500 or fewer employees for all industries in both the Retail Trade and Wholesale Trade Sectors.

[138] The 509 count of employee-based size standards includes the use of a combination of number of employees and barrel per day refining capacity for petroleum refineries.

[139] The annual receipts of a concern which has been in business for less than three complete fiscal years is determined by dividing the total receipts for the period the concern has been in business by the number of weeks in business, multiplied by 52. See 13 C.F.R. §121.104.

[140] U.S. Small Business Administration, "Table of Small Business Size Standards," July 22, 2013, at http://www.sba.gov/content/table-small-business-size-standards.

[141] Ibid.

[142] P.L. 99-272, the Consolidated Omnibus Budget Reconciliation Act of 1985 (Title XVIII, Section 18016) inserted a requirement that notwithstanding any other provision of law, an agricultural enterprise shall be deemed to be a small business concern if it, including its affiliates, has annual receipts not in excess of $500,000. P.L. 106-554, the Consolidated Appropriations Act, 2001 (Title VIII, Section 806(b)), substituted "$750,000" for "$500,000."

- most health care industries have an upper limit of either $7.0 million or $14.0 million in average annual sales or receipts;

- most social assistance industries have an upper limit of $10.0 million in average annual sales or receipts;

- most professional, scientific, and technical service industries have an upper limit of $14.0 million in average annual sales or receipts, but range from $7.0 million to $35.5 million;

- there is considerable variation within the transportation and warehousing industrial sector (e.g., all 11 transit and ground passenger transportation industries have an upper limit of $14.0 million in average annual sales or receipts, the 6 truck transportation and 4 transportation warehousing and storage industries have an upper limit of $25.5 million in average annual sales or receipts, 7 transportation industries have an upper limit of 500 employees, 8 transportation industries have an upper limit of 1,500 employees, and the remaining industries in this sector have an upper limit ranging from $7.0 million to $35.5 million in average annual sales or receipts); and

- most finance and insurance industries have an upper limit of $35.5 million in average annual sales or receipts.

The SBA also applies a $500 million average asset limit (as reported in the firm's four quarterly financial statements for the preceding year) to determine eligibility in five finance industries: commercial banks, saving institutions, credit unions, other depository credit intermediation, and credit card issuing.[143]

As mentioned previously, the SBA is currently using eight receipt-based size standards when establishing or reviewing size standards. The SBA has argued that reducing the number of receipt-based size standards, from 31 to 8, will simplify the management and use of size standards and provide "greater consistency in size standards among industries that are similar in their economic characteristics."[144]

The SBA's decision to reduce the number of receipt-based size standards and to use a common size standard for closely related industries when establishing or approving industry size standards raised the possibility of establishing or approving a size standard that may not be directly supported by its economic assessment of that industrial classification. For example, in the final rule issued for Professional, Technical, and Scientific Services (Sector 54), on February 10, 2012, the SBA argued that "it should continue to maintain similar or comparable size standards among the surveying and mapping industries and the architectural and engineering service industries."[145] As a result,

> although the industry data point to a size standard higher than $14 million for NAICS 541360 and lower than $14 million for NAICS 541370, SBA believes a common size

---

[143] U.S. Small Business Administration, "Table of Small Business Size Standards," July 22, 2013, at http://www.sba.gov/content/table-small-business-size-standards.

[144] U.S. Small Business Administration, Office of Government Contracting and Business Development, "SBA Size Standards Methodology," April 2009, p. 22, at http://www.sba.gov/sites/default/files/size_standards_methodology.pdf.

[145] U.S. Small Business Administration, "Small Business Size Standards: Professional, Technical, and Scientific Services," 77 *Federal Register* 7498, February 10, 2012.

standard of $14 million is more appropriate than establishing two very different size standards for the two very similar types of industries, because (1) it represents a significant increase to the current size standard, as the commenters desired and (2) it maintains the historical common size standard between mapping and surveying services and architecture and engineering services.[146]

H.R. 3987, the Small Business Protection Act of 2012, introduced on February 8, 2012, and ordered to be reported by the House Committee on Small Business on March 21, 2012, addressed the SBA's recent practice of combining size standards within industrial groups to promote greater consistency for industries that have similar economic characteristics.

The bill would have authorized the SBA's Administrator to "establish or approve a single size standard for a grouping of four digit North American Industrial Classification codes only if the Administrator makes publicly available, not later than the date on which such size standard is established or approved, a justification demonstrating that such size standard is appropriate for each individual industry classification included in the grouping."[147] The bill would have required the SBA's Administrator

> to provide a detailed description of the industry for which the new size standard is proposed; an analysis of the competitive environment for that industry; the approach the Administrator used to develop the proposed standard including the source of all data used to develop the proposed rulemaking; and the anticipated effect of the proposed rulemaking on the industry, including the number of concerns not currently considered small that would be considered small under the proposed rulemaking and the number of concerns currently considered small that would be deemed other than small under the proposed rulemaking.[148]

P.L. 112-239, the National Defense Authorization Act for Fiscal Year 2013, which became law on January 2, 2013, included these provisions. The Senate's version of the bill did not include these provisions, but the conference report accompanying the bill (H.R. 4310), which was agreed to by the House on December 20, 2012, and by the Senate on December 21, 2012, included them.

Other Federal Agency Size Standards

Many federal statutes provide special considerations for small businesses. For example, small businesses are provided preferences through set-asides and sole source awards in federal contracting and pay lower fees to apply for patents and trademarks.[149] In most instances, businesses are required to meet the SBA's size standards to be considered a small business. However, in some cases, the underlying statute defines the eligibility criteria for defining a small

---

[146] Ibid.

[147] H.R. 3987, the Small Business Protection Act of 2012, Section 2, Small Business Concern Size Standards.

[148] Ibid.

[149] The federal government has a goal of awarding at least 23% of all small business eligible federal government procurement contracts to small businesses, including 5% for small disadvantaged businesses, 5% for women-owned small businesses, 3% for small businesses owned by service-disabled veterans, and 3% for small businesses located in a HUBZone. See U.S. General Services Administration, Federal Procurement Data System – Next Generation, "Small Business Goaling Reports," at https://www.fpds.gov/fpdsng_cms/index.php/en/reports. For further information and analysis concerning federal contracting preferences for small businesses see CRS Report R41268, *Small Business Administration HUBZone Program*, by Robert Jay Dilger.

business. In other cases, the statute authorizes the implementing agency to make those determinations.

Under current law, a federal agency that decides that it would like to exercise its authority to establish its own size standard through the federal rulemaking process is required to, among other things, (1) undertake an initial regulatory flexibility analysis to determine the potential impact of the proposed rule on small businesses, (2) transmit a copy of the initial regulatory flexibility analysis to the SBA's Chief Counsel for Advocacy for comment, and (3) publish the agency's response to any comments filed by the SBA's Chief Counsel for Advocacy in response to the proposed rule and a detailed statement of any change made to the proposed rule in the final rule as a result of those comments.[150] In addition, the federal agency must provide public notice of the proposed rule and an opportunity for the public to comment on the proposed rule, typically through the publication of an advanced notice of proposed rulemaking in the *Federal Register* and notification of interested small businesses and related organizations.[151] Also, prior to issuing the final rule, the federal agency must have the approval of the SBA's Administrator.[152] Under current practice, the SBA's Administrator, through the SBA's Office of Size Standards, consults with the SBA's Office of Advocacy prior to making a final decision concerning such requests.[153] The Office of Advocacy is an independent office within the SBA.

During the 112th Congress, H.R. 585, the Small Business Size Standard Flexibility Act of 2011, was reported by the House Committee on Small Business on November 16, 2011, by a vote of 13 to 8. The bill would have retained the SBA's Administrator's authority to develop size standards for programs under the Small Business Act of 1953 (as amended) and the Small Business Investment Act of 1958 (as amended). The Office of Chief Counsel for Advocacy would have assumed the SBA Administrator's authority to approve or disapprove a size standard proposed by a federal agency if it deviates from the SBA's size standards.[154]

Advocates of splitting the SBA Administrator's small business size standards' authority between the Office of Chief Counsel for Advocacy and the SBA's Administrator argued that

> Should an agency wish to draft a regulation that adopts a size standard different from the one already adopted by the Administrator in regulations implementing the Small Business Act,

---

[150] 5 U.S.C. 601; 5 U.S.C. 603; and 5 U.S.C. 604.

[151] 15 U.S.C. 632.

[152] Ibid. The SBA reports "that there have been approximately 25 requests by other agencies under the authority of amended §3 of the Small Business Act since the date of amendment in 1992." See U.S. Congress, House Committee on Small Business, *Small Business Size Standard Flexibility Act of 2011*, report to accompany H.R. 585, 112th Cong., 2nd sess., November 16, 2011, H.Rept. 112-288 (Washington: GPO, 2011), p. 7.

[153] Representative Sam Graves, "Full Committee Hearing, Lifting the Weight of Regulations: Growing Jobs By Reducing Regulatory Burdens (III. H.R. 585—Small Business Size Standard Flexibility Act of 2011)," letter to House Committee on Small Business, June 8, 2011, p. 44, at http://smbiz.house.gov/UploadedFiles/6-15_Memo.pdf; U.S. Congressional Budget Office, "Congressional Budget Office Cost Estimate: H.R. 585—Small Business Size Standard Flexibility Act of 2011," p. 2, at http://www.cbo.gov/ftpdocs/124xx/doc12449/hr585.pdf; and U.S. Congress, House Committee on Small Business, *Small Business Size Standard Flexibility Act of 2011*, report to accompany H.R. 585, 112th Cong., 2nd sess., November 16, 2011, H.Rept. 112-288 (Washington: GPO, 2011), pp. 6-8. Also, see 13 C.F.R §121.901-903.

[154] U.S. Congressional Budget Office, "Congressional Budget Office Cost Estimate: H.R. 585—Small Business Size Standard Flexibility Act of 2011," p. 2, at http://www.cbo.gov/ftpdocs/124xx/doc12449/hr585.pdf; and H.Rept. 112-288, the Business Size Standard Flexibility Act of 2011. CBO has estimated that the Office of Advocacy would ultimately need 10 additional staff positions to implement its new authority; and that the bill would cost $6 million over the 2012-2016 period.

the agency must obtain approval of the Administrator. However, that requires the Administrator to have a complete understanding of the regulatory regime of that other act—knowledge usually outside the expertise of the SBA. However, the Office of the Chief Counsel for Advocacy, an independent office within the SBA, represents the interests of small businesses in rulemaking proceedings (as part of its responsibility to monitor agency compliance with the Regulatory Flexibility Act, 5 U.S.C. 601-12, (RFA)) does have such expertise. Therefore, it is logical to transfer the limited function on determining size standards of small businesses for purposes other than the Small Business Act and Small Business Investment Act of 1958 to the Office of the Chief Counsel for Advocacy....

the Administrator is not the proper official to determine size standards for purposes of other agencies' regulatory activities. The Administrator is not fluent with the vast array of federal regulatory programs, is not in constant communication with small entities that might be affected by another federal agency's regulatory regime, and does not have the analytical expertise to assess the regulatory impact of a particular size standard on small entities. Furthermore, the Administrator's standards are: very inclusive, not developed to comport with other agencies' regulatory regimes, and lack sufficient granularity to examine the impact of a proposed rule on a spectrum of small businesses.[155]

Opponents argued that

When an agency is seeking to use a size standard other than those approved by the SBA, the agency may consult with the Office of Advocacy. Such consultation is sensible, as the Office of Advocacy has significant knowledge of the regulatory environment outside of the canon of SBA law. However, the SBA's Office of Size Standards, with its historical involvement, expertise, and staff resources in this area, remains the appropriate entity to approve such size standards....

While the legislation permits the SBA to continue to approve size standards for its enabling statutes, it removes SBA's authority to do so for other statutes. The result would be to create a duplicate size standard authority in both the SBA and the Office of Advocacy. Both the SBA and the Office of Advocacy would have personnel who would analyze and evaluate size standards. Through the bifurcation of these responsibilities, taxpayers would effectively be forgoing the economies of scale that are currently enjoyed by the operation of a single Office of Size Standards in the SBA....

Having two such entities that have the same mission is not a transfer of function, but an inefficient and duplicative reorganization.... Instead of having one central office, there will now be two—further muddling small businesses' relationship with the federal government.[156]

Congressional Policy Options

Historically, the SBA has relied on economic analysis of market conditions within each industry to define eligibility for small business assistance. On several occasions in its history, the SBA attempted to revise its small business size standards in a comprehensive manner. However, because (1) the Small Business Act provides leeway in how the SBA is to define small business;

---

[155] U.S. Congress, House Committee on Small Business, *Small Business Size Standard Flexibility Act of 2011*, report to accompany H.R. 585, 112th Cong., 2nd sess., November 16, 2011, H.Rept. 112-288 (Washington: GPO, 2011), p. 6.
[156] Ibid., p. 14.

(2) there is no consensus on the economic factors that should be used in defining small business; (3) federal agencies have generally opposed size standards that might adversely affect their pool of available small business contractors; and (4) the SBA's initial size standards provided program eligibility to nearly all businesses, the SBA's efforts to undertake a comprehensive reassessment of its size standards met with resistance. Firms that might lose eligibility objected. Federal agencies also objected. As a result, in each instance, the SBA's comprehensive revisions were not fully implemented.

It remains to be seen how the requirement to conduct a detailed review of at least one-third of the SBA's industry size standards every 18 months, which was imposed by P.L. 111-240, the Small Business Jobs Act of 2010, will affect the SBA's current, ongoing review of each NAICS Sector in a sequential fashion. For example, the SBA may find it necessary to increase the number of OSS staff to meet the new requirement.

In the meantime, the SBA continues to adjust its monetary based size standards for inflation at least once every five years, or more frequently if inflationary circumstances warrant, to prevent firms from losing their small business eligibility solely due to the effects of inflation. The last adjustment for inflation took place in 2008.[157] The SBA also continues to review size standards within specific industries whenever it determines that market conditions within that industry have changed.

Congress has several options related to the SBA's ongoing review of its size standards. For example, as part of its oversight of the SBA, Congress can wait for the agency to issue its proposed rule before providing input or establish a dialogue with the agency, either at the staff level or with Members involved directly, prior to the issuance of its proposed rule. Historically, Congress has tended to wait for the SBA to issue proposed rules concerning its size standards before providing input, essentially deferring to the agency's expertise in the technical and methodological issues involved in determining where to draw the line between small and large firms. Congress has then tended to respond to the SBA's proposed rules concerning its size standards after taking into consideration current economic conditions and input received from the SBA and affected industries.

Waiting for the SBA to issue its proposed rule concerning its size standards before providing congressional input has both advantages and disadvantages. It provides the advantage of insulating the proposed rule from charges that it is influenced by political factors. It also has the advantage of respecting the separation of powers and responsibilities of the executive and legislative branches. However, it has the disadvantage of heightening the prospects for miscommunication, false expectations, and wasted effort, as evidenced by past proposed rules concerning the SBA's size standards that were either rejected outright, or withdrawn, after facing congressional opposition.

Another policy option that has not received much congressional attention in recent years, but which Congress may choose to address, is the targeting of the SBA's resources. When the SBA reviews its size standards, it focuses on the competitive nature of the industry under review, with the goal of removing eligibility of firms that are considered large, or dominant, in that industry. There has been relatively little discussion of the costs and benefits of undertaking those reviews

---

[157] U.S. Small Business Administration, "Small Business Size Standards: Inflation Adjustment to Size Standards, Business Loan Programs, and Disaster Assistance Program," 73 *Federal Register* 41237-41254, July 18, 2008.

with the goal of targeting SBA resources to small businesses that are struggling to remain competitive. GAO recommended this approach in 1978 and Roger Rosenberger, then SBA's associate administrator for policy, planning, and budgeting, testified at a congressional hearing in 1979 that it was debatable whether the SBA should provide any assistance to any of the businesses within industries where "smaller firms are flourishing."[158]

Revising the SBA's size standards using this more targeted approach would likely reduce the number of firms eligible for assistance. It would also present the possibility of increasing available benefits to eligible small firms in those industries deemed "mixed" or "concentrated" by the SBA without necessarily increasing overall program costs. Perhaps because previous proposals that would result in a reduction in the number of firms eligible for assistance have met with resistance, this alternative approach to determining program eligibility has not received serious consideration in recent years. Nonetheless, it remains an option available to Congress should it decide to change current policy.

Author Contact Information

Robert Jay Dilger
Senior Specialist in American National Government
rdilger@crs.loc.gov, 7-3110

---

[158] U.S. Congress, House Committee on Small Business, Subcommittee on General Oversight and Minority Enterprise, *Size Standards for Small Business*, hearing, 96th Cong., 1st sess., July 10, 1979 (Washington: GPO, 1979), p. 28.

www.ingramcontent.com/pod-product-compliance
Lightning Source LLC
Chambersburg PA
CBHW081804170526

45167CB00008B/3315